Building Up Jerusalem

Lessons for the Church Today

Gilbert Vega

TEACH Services, Inc.
PUBLISHING
www.TEACHServices.com • (800) 367-1844

World rights reserved. This book or any portion thereof may not be copied or reproduced in any form or manner whatever, except as provided by law, without the written permission of the publisher, except by a reviewer who may quote brief passages in a review.

The author assumes full responsibility for the accuracy of all facts and quotations as cited in this book. The opinions expressed in this book are the author's personal views and interpretations, and do not necessarily reflect those of the publisher.

This book is provided with the understanding that the publisher is not engaged in giving spiritual, legal, medical, or other professional advice. If authoritative advice is needed, the reader should seek the counsel of a competent professional.

Copyright © 2022 Gilbert Vega
Copyright © 2022 TEACH Services, Inc.
ISBN-13: 978-1-4796-1370-0 (Paperback)
ISBN-13: 978-1-4796-1371-7 (ePub)
Library of Congress Control Number: 2021914507

New International Version (NIV)
Scripture quotations marked NIV are taken from THE HOLY BIBLE, NEW INTERNATIONAL VERSION®, NIV® Copyright © 1973, 1978, 1984, 2011 by Biblica, Inc.® Used by permission. All rights reserved worldwide.

Revised Standard Version (RSV)
Revised Standard Version of the Bible, copyright © 1946, 1952, and 1971 the Division of Christian Education of the National Council of the Churches of Christ in the United States of America. Used by permission. All rights reserved.

New King James Version (NKJV)
All scripture quotations, unless otherwise indicated, are taken from the New King James Version®. Copyright © 1982 by Thomas Nelson. Used by permission. All rights reserved.

Modern English Version (MEV)
The Holy Bible, Modern English Version. Copyright © 2014 by Military Bible Association. Published and distributed by Charisma House.

Published by

www.TEACHServices.com • (800) 367-1844

Table of Contents

Introduction v
  1. Historical Overview. 7
  2. Personalities of the Second Exodus. 13
  3. The Exile 23
  4. A Remnant. 30
  5. Crossing the Desert. 39
  6. Challenges to the Construction 47
  7. Completion of the Temple 55
  8. Building the Walls 61
  9. Enemies 71
  10. Unequally Yoked (Defining Who You Are…) 80
  11. Populating the City 84
  12. Prophetic Guidance 92
  13. Revival and Reformation 97
Afterthoughts 106
Appendix A: Chronology 108
Bibliography. 111

Introduction

The fall of the city of Jerusalem and the captivity that followed was a crushing blow to the city and the psyche of the entire Jewish state. Popular in the minds of the people was the notion that Jerusalem would stand forever. Zion was God's "holy mountain," and as such, Yahweh would protect the city that He had chosen to house His temple. The lovely and imposing structure was the pride and joy of every Israelite. Therefore, when the invading army of a pagan nation conquered the city and plundered the temple, it was an incomprehensible event. Furthermore, the king, a direct descendant from David, watched as his sons were killed before his eyes were gouged and he was taken to Babylon in shackles. As thousands of Jews were taken into captivity, there were troublesome and lingering questions:

- What would the future hold for Israel?
- Would there be a restoration to its former glory?
- Had God rejected Israel as His chosen people?

Such were the questions hurling in the minds of most Israelites in 586 BC.

However, the answers to such questions had already been penned by the prophets. There *would be* a restoration, and

Jerusalem would once again vibrate with life. As predicted, a remnant did return, and Jerusalem was repopulated by returning Jews.

The re-settlement of Jerusalem was a gradual process that spanned various decades. An initial wave of settlers arrived in 536 BC and was able to finish rebuilding the temple in 515 BC. The next major event in the restoration process was rebuilding the walls of the city, and that took place in 444 BC.

The objective of this work is to relive the historical narrative of the brave individuals who took it upon themselves to build up an entire city. For the purpose of the narrative, I will be highlighting the two major events cited above: rebuilding the temple and the walls of the city. Though these events were separated by seventy-one years, I will treat them as one pivotal event: the restoration of Jerusalem. Secondarily, we will extrapolate applicable lessons for the contemporary church in our task of preparing a people for the kingdom of God.

Are you ready? Come, let's build up Jerusalem—let's build up the church, together.

Chapter 1
Historical Overview

The summer of 605 BC was not a fun-filled summer for Jerusalem and its environs. As usual, the watchmen on the walls of Jerusalem were scouting the horizon for any potential danger. Habitually, they fix their eyes on any visible stirring in the distance. That summer day in July, amidst the blowing dust, they glimpse an approaching army. It is the mighty Babylonian army feared by all nations. Nebuchadnezzar, the young and daring prince of Babylon, commanded the troops, which had already wrought chaos in their path. The imposing fighting force had been on a successful swing through Palestine and had already subjugated Lachish, an extremely well-fortified city. Now, that fierce fighting machine was approaching the City of David.

God and geography had placed Judah in a prime locale. It was located between the two superpowers of the era: Egypt to the southwest and Babylon to the northeast. Because of its unique location, it often had to choose sides in the all-too-common wars to determine who would yield political hegemony over the region. For the past few years, Judah had established a political arrangement with Egypt in return for military assistance. However, a couple of months earlier, the Babylonian army had decisively defeated the Egyptians at Carchemish and had entered Palestine. That immediately translated into trouble for Judah—an ally of Necho, Egypt's defeated pharaoh.

In July of 605 BC, Nebuchadnezzar's troops placed a siege around Jerusalem. All communications by the city with the outside world were cut off. As such, there was no food supply entering the city. A siege was meant to suffocate a city and lead to a speedy surrender without major loss of man or material. It was only a matter of time when the emaciated citizenry would demand its leaders to surrender to the mighty army from the north. By August 605 BC, the city surrendered, and the Babylonians began to divide and haul the spoils of victory. Although Nebuchadnezzar hastily abandoned the scene, due to news from Babylon regarding the death of his father Nabopolassar, the well-disciplined Babylonian forces remained to claim yet another victory.

The conquering cohorts entered the city and hastily subjugated its weakened population. The invaders followed a practice common to the era; that of transplanting many of the conquered peoples to other regions within the kingdom. Thus, a significant number of the city's elite citizens were rounded up and dispersed within the Babylonian Empire.

Those taken were typically the *crème de la crème,* the young and gifted. It was the first of three major deportations that the proud Jewish state would have to endure in its confrontation with the city-state by the Fertile Crescent. Needless to say, it was a humiliating defeat for any city, but even more so for Jerusalem, in light of its history and theological outlook on the role of Zion (see Ps. 125:1). Nevertheless, King Jehoiakim (609–598 BC), was left on the throne; though now his land was a vassal state to the Neo-Babylonian Empire, to whom he had sworn loyalty.

However, Jehoiakim was not a cooperative partner. His loyalty lasted while the mighty sword of Babylon was latently visible. By 601 BC, Egypt had a resurgence of power and was ready to make another geo-political statement in the region. In a non-decisive battle, the Babylonians took heavy losses, and that emboldened Jehoiakim to switch loyalties back to Egypt. Since Nebuchadnezzar was busy with other affairs, he did not immediately respond to such an affront. However, he did send a small force to harass Judah and destabilize the region until a larger force could be sent. In December of 598 BC, Jehoiakim died in Jerusalem. It is not clear whether he died or was killed by those who blamed him as the culprit for much of the city's travail (see 2 Kings 24:1–8; Jer. 22:18).

The next occupant of the throne of Judah was a teenager—eighteen-year-old Jehoiachin (598–597 BC). The state of affairs was chaotic. As the large Babylonian army approached the city, differing parties had developed within the leadership strata. One group espoused a pacifist ideology and wanted to surrender, whereas others called for bold and decisive opposition to the Babylonian masters.

However, Zion was disheartened and nearly leaderless. On March 16, 597 BC, Judah's capital surrendered to the Babylonians. The young king, his wives, the queen mother, courtiers, high officials, and many leading citizens were taken to Babylon (see 2 Kings 24). As many as 10,000 talented young people of the land were rounded up and marched off to the northeast. The future prophet Ezekiel was among those sent to exile.

Next, Nebuchadnezzar placed on the throne Zedekiah (597–586 BC), an uncle to Jehoiachin and someone whom the king of Babylon hand-picked. Again, the political strife within the nation and especially in Jerusalem dictated the events. There was an ever-present anti-Babylon party that sought to sway Zedekiah. His ambivalence forbade him to step in and make critical decisions at such a crucial time. Eventually, he succumbed to the anti-Babylonian party and trusted in forthcoming help from Egypt. Soon Babylon became aware of the rebellion and took measures. This time Nebuchadnezzar came personally and, in anger, laid siege to the city. It was the year 588 BC. The extended siege generated the expected chaos within the city—famine, disease, and divisive clamoring. On July 19 of 586, the invaders were able to breach the walls and enter the city. A month later, Nebuzaradan, Nebuchadnezzar's commander, was ordered to burn many of the leading buildings and tear down its walls.

God handed all of them over to Nebuchadnezzar.

> He carried to Babylon all the articles from the temple of God, both large and small, and the treasures of the LORD's temple and the treasures of the king and his officials. They set fire to God's temple and broke down the wall of Jerusalem; they burned all the palaces and destroyed everything of value there. He carried into exile to Babylon the remnant, who escaped from the sword, and they became servants to him and his sons until the kingdom of Persia came to power. (2 Chron. 36:17–20, NIV)

Again, a good portion of the nobility was rounded up and taken to Babylon. Others were executed. It was then that the temple, that impressive monument to Yahweh, would be destroyed. Having looted its riches, the new lords of the city wanted to destroy that unique symbol of nationhood. Such a monumental building, so rich in history and hallowed by divine manifestation, was no more. It had stood for more than three centuries, but now its end had come. The royal palace and most of the city dwellings were similarly burned to the ground. The walls, which had sheltered the city for centuries, were likewise leveled.

Such a monumental building, so rich in history and hallowed by divine manifestation, was no more.

The events of July and August of 586 BC, transformed the City of David into a heap of dirt and dust. Death and destruction were felt and seen everywhere. The charred remains of the city brought the prophet Jeremiah to utter anguish. Indeed, there were many reasons to cry: the monarchy had come to an end, and the holy city lay in ruins. It was definitely a time to wail for the daughter of Zion (see 2 Kings 25:8–12; Jer. 52:12–16; Book of Lamentations; Ps. 74; 79).

For the time being, the history and ethos of the Jewish nation would, by necessity, take place outside of Judean soil. Babylon and its cities would be their home for the next seven decades. A distance of 900 miles would separate the Jews from Judah and Jerusalem. Once again, they would be strangers in a heathen nation. The ominous warnings of Moses, now a reality, must have sent shivers down their spines (see Deut. 28:15–68).

For most Jews, the fall of Jerusalem was their worst nightmare. It was simply unimaginable, extremely unbearable. All of their lives, they had been schooled in the philosophy that the temple was God's footstool and thus, unshakeable (see 1 Chron. 28:2). Above all, to add misery to injury, it was the despised Babylonians who had crushed their infants and violated their women. That such an odious people had literally dismantled their city-state and turned their theology upside down was downright agonizing. It was excruciating to have their beloved city destroyed, but on top of that, they were no longer a nation—only a throng of sheep scattered throughout the Neo-Babylonian Empire. Reality check: Judah as an independent state was no more.

Finding themselves as exiles on foreign soil, after eight centuries of national autonomy, was indeed bitter medicine. It was the cruelest of paradigm shifts: they had lost their independence and now served heathen rulers.

Though the future was extremely grim, many followed the counsel of the prophet Jeremiah and tried to gain a sense of normalcy in light of their plight (see Jer. 29:4–5). Understanding that their stay in Babylon would be longer than expected, they set out to make the most of their precarious visit.

Some Jews entered government service. Others worked for the state in a semi-serfdom status. Yet, others were allowed to set up shop and become merchants. In the course of time, a number of them prospered and became wealthy.

However, all of them were in harmony in the belief that Yahweh had chastised them, and thus, their captivity was God-directed. In spite of their dire lot, a remnant among them was certain that Heaven would revisit them and act on their behalf. To their unbelief, the much-maligned denunciations of Jeremiah had been fulfilled to the letter. However, the weeping prophet also shared visions of a remnant returning from Babylon. Those writings, along with those of Isaiah, were eagerly studied and birthed hope (see Jer. 25:11–12).

Chapter 2
Personalities of the Second Exodus

Daniel: Daniel was part of the first wave of exiles which were removed from Jerusalem in 605 BC. By way of a dramatic series of events, he was brought before King Nebuchadnezzar and promoted to be the leading counselor to the king. In that position, he served the monarch till 562 BC, when the aged ruler passed away.

The years that followed the death of the king, were ones of political wrangling by various factions seeking the seat of power. Eventually, by 556 BC, the prevailing figure was Nabonidus. Nabonidus was not entirely interested in the daily affairs of the palace, and so he wandered off to different parts of the kingdom to pursue his interests in nature. To carry on the business of the state, his son Belshazzar was placed in charge.

However, Belshazzar was not much better at governing and used his position to live it up. It was while engaged in one of his state banquets that the Persians approached the city. The invading Persian forces ingeniously found their way into the city and crashed the party. That very night Belshazzar was killed, Babylon fell, and Persia was propelled into the status of an empire. Cyrus placed Darius in charge of Babylon, and a new page of Middle Eastern geopolitics had begun. These dramatic and momentous events took place on the night of October 12, 539 BC.

The very event of the fall of Babylon ignited in the mind of Daniel a possibility for his exiled fellow Jews. Thus, he began a thorough and methodical search of the prophetic writings of the pre-exile prophets to assess their prophetic insights.

Isaiah, Jeremiah, and Ezekiel had all penned prophetic utterances concerning the return of Israel to its homeland. The aged prophet was rewarded in his quest. In his search, he took special notice of the writings of Jeremiah, who had indeed recorded that the captivity would last for seventy years (see Jer. 25:12). Daniel was greatly pleased as he realized that sixty-eight of the seventy years had already elapsed. The captivity would soon be over. Needless to say, that affirmation sent waves of hope through the ranks of the captives. The end was in sight. Soon God would make a path back to the "glorious land." They would simply have to wait for Yahweh to intervene on their behalf.[1]

Cyrus: In the fall of 538 BC, Darius dies, and Cyrus as the *de jure* king of the empire, assumes direct involvement in the direction of the city of Babylon. Henceforth, he will be known as Cyrus the Great for his numerous accomplishments. Unbelievably, Daniel is retained to work for the new Medo-Persian Empire. That provides him with a front seat to the stage of world history. Surprisingly, Cyrus turns out to be a benevolent and wise magistrate. One of his unique policies would directly impact the Jewish exiles. It is likely that Daniel may have shown Cyrus Isaiah's prophecy, where the king was mentioned by name—two hundred years prior to his ascension (see Isa. 44:28; 45:1).

One radical shift of policy under Persian rule was that of returning conquered peoples to their former homelands. Since he

---

[1] C. Mervyn Maxwell, *God Cares*, 2 Vols: *The Message of Daniel for you and your Family* (Boise, Idaho: Pacific Press Publishing Association, 1981), Vol. 1, 200–203.

had inherited a large Jewish population within the empire, Cyrus considered the matter and made a decision. He decreed that the Jews would be allowed to return to Jerusalem. In addition, he opened an account in the royal treasury so that expenses would be covered by the monarchy. It was almost unbelievable that a conquering king would be allowing repatriation for the Jews, and furthermore, that the national coffers would bear the brunt of the relocation (see Ezra 6:1–5).

There were three major phases in the repatriation of the Jews, which scholars have nicknamed the Second Exodus. The very first group was led by Zerubbabel, and it began its westward trek in 536 BC. Nearly eighty years later, in 457 BC, a second band of exiles departed from Susa under the leadership of Ezra. The third contingent of returnees departed from Susa thirteen years later, 444 BC, and it was led by Nehemiah.[2]

Zerubbabel: Not much is known of Zerubbabel, and yet we cannot ignore his pivotal role in the process that culminated in the resettlement of Jerusalem. He was of noble origin and probably was a man of means. Indeed, he was a blood descendant of King Jehoiachin (see Matt. 1:12). All indications are that he was born in exile and was a prosperous individual. When Cyrus allowed the Jews to return to Palestine, he surfaces as the political leader, which sheds light on his status and eminence within the exiled community. Since the number of people traveling back to Jerusalem was nearly 50,000, and Zerubbabel was empowered with their safety, one has to conclude that his leadership abilities among the exiles were highly esteemed.

---

[2]The Jews returned to Jerusalem in significant numbers on three separate occasions. The first one took place in 536 BC, and that was led by Zerubbabel. A second wave arrived in 457 BC, and it was led by Ezra, while a third contingent arrived thirteen years later in 444 BC, and that one was led by Nehemiah. See Charles R. Swindoll, *Hand Me Another Brick: How Effective Leaders Motivate Themselves and Others* (Nashville, TN: Thomas Nelson, Inc. 1998), 8. The number of returnees—including servants—that traveled with Zerubbabel was nearly 50,000. while those that returned with Ezra were about 8,000. The number of exiles who returned with Nehemiah is not specified, and for that reason, scholars believe that it was a much smaller number than the previous waves. See *Seventh-day Adventist Bible Commentary*, 11 vols., F. D. Nichol, ed. (Washington, DC: Review and Herald Publishing Association, 1953–1957), Vol. 3, 375–376.

One cannot underestimate the emotional and spiritual value of the enterprise. They were leaving the "rivers of Babylon" and heading towards their ancestral home. However, the vast majority of those returning had very little knowledge of the terrain of Palestine. Nevertheless, one can assume that they all had heard nostalgic stories from family members concerning their beloved Judah and Zion. Consequently, traveling to the land was a highly emotional experience, yet one which did not lack danger.

In the narrative of the resettlement of Jerusalem, the name of Zerubbabel stands out as an unwavering personality. Although his task was a difficult one, one senses that he was a cautious individual who moved about very deliberately. There is no account that mentions him conducting or proposing any daring project. Upon arriving at Palestine, common-sense practices were put in place, and the resettlement project was off to a good start. Aside from surviving and making a living in the new land, the reconstruction of the temple was Zerubbabel's main objective. When motivation and zeal waned, and the enterprise seemed at a stalemate, it seems that he lacked the motivational charisma to rally the disheartened settlers forward. God, however, raised two prophets to buoy his spirit. At that critical period of the enterprise, he was sustained and uplifted by the ministry of Haggai and Zechariah.

Zerubbabel had lasting power. He was appointed governor in 537 BC, and twenty-two years later, 515 BC, he was still at his post. Given the challenging circumstances under which he had to labor, his long tenure underscores how much he was valued. It is a testimony to his personality and the respect he had garnered within the community.

Joshua: Someone who came in the first wave of settlers in 536 BC, and worked hand in hand with Zerubbabel, was Joshua. Nothing is known of his early years. He was a Levite and a priest. His title in the leadership rung was that of high priest. Thus, he had a very prominent and distinctive role among the leading personalities. Since there was no temple, his role of high priest was somewhat limited. So, in reality, his main function was that of being the top spiritual leader on the compound. In 520 BC, when Haggai burst onto the scene and made it his mission to jumpstart the temple project, one of the persons whom he addressed by name was Joshua (see Hag. 1:12–14). Joshua responded with passion and dedication to the challenge proposed by the prophet. Thus, it can be said that because of his reaction and that of Zerubbabel, Joshua was partly instrumental in reigniting the construction project.

His ministry expanded a period of history that was very challenging for the returnees. One can guess that because of the malaise displayed by many of the people, at times, he may have felt discouraged. One senses that because both Haggai and Zechariah pressed him to stay the course and forge ahead on the temple reconstruction (see Hag. 2:4; Zech. 3:1–10). One hopes that he was present when the temple was completed (515 BC) since that would have brought him an enormous amount of gratification.

Haggai: The initial enthusiasm of the returnees to rebuild the temple waned not long after their arrival in 536 BC. There were a number of factors which derailed the promising project:

- The constant harassment by neighboring peoples was an issue that drained nerves and energy.
- The assessment by the older crowd that anything they built would be totally inferior to the glory of the first temple.
- The need for many of them to build their homes and raise crops for mere survival.
- The lack of a charismatic leader who would dislodge them from their malaise.

In 535 BC, there was abundant zeal and optimism. However, once the project was no longer at center stage, their energy waned and was directed at their individual homes and farms. The temple project would have united them and provided them with a common goal. Sadly, though, that did not occur. Therefore, God moved to raise a prophet that would stir the people to recapture the vision. The man chosen was Haggai. It was the year 520 BC.

Haggai's background is quite sketchy. Two interesting details of his life may be inferred from his book. Firstly, he may have been a young lad in 586 BC and may have been among those who had seen the glory of the first temple. Some scholars deduce that from the following text: "Who is left among you that saw this house in its former glory? How do you see it now? Is it not in your sight as nothing?" (Hag. 2:3, RSV). If that is a fact, he would have been advanced in age by the time he receives the prophetic unction.

Secondly, he may have been a priest. That view has been toyed about because of an illustration where he postulates hypothetical questions to a priest (see Hag. 2:10–14). If those two assumptions are correct, he was a man of position and clout. It would also explain the degree to which his ministry was enthusiastically received. Whether a priest or not, he was instrumental in bolstering the morale of the people and mobilizing them back towards the project. A testament to his effectiveness is the brevity of his ministry—only four months—in light of his transformational role in the history of the exiles.

Zechariah: As with Haggai, little is known about Zechariah's personal background. There is a consensus among scholars that he was a priest and descended from a priestly family. That is based on his statement that he hailed from the lineage of Iddo (see Zech. 1:1), and such was the name of a leading priest who returned with Zerubbabel (see Neh. 12:1–4). His familiarity and interest in matters relating to the temple also lends some weight to that hunch. It is presumed that he was born in exile.

The ministry of Haggai and Zechariah addressed the returned Jews as the remnant of Israel.

Zechariah was a contemporary to Haggai. The tenor of his message is aimed at Zerubbabel and Joshua, the political and spiritual leaders of the enterprise. The first eight chapters of the book address similar issues as those tackled by Haggai. However, unlike Haggai, he moves beyond the present issues of the restoration and portrays in chapters 9–14, a futuristic view of Jerusalem and Israel. Allusions to the future Messiah run deep in his writing.

The ministry of Haggai and Zechariah addressed the returned Jews as the remnant of Israel. Such affirmations could have been politically risky, but they enunciated and served to instill within the struggling community the needed courage to move forward. With their encouragement, the construction of the temple was reinitiated in 520 BC and completed five years hence, in 515 BC.

Ezra: The evidence weighs heavily on the side that he was born in captivity. He led a second wave of Jews that made their way back to Palestine in 457 BC. Ezra's trek took place about eighty years after the initial group led by Zerubbabel. It was in the seventh year of his reign (565–423 BC) that King Artaxerxes commissioned Ezra to lead a second wave of settlers to Palestine.[3] His overall mission was to establish civil and religious administration amongst the feeble settlers who had gone with the first wave of settlement some eighty years earlier. Artaxerxes' initiative offered Ezra a number of prerogatives, which he was to utilize in his path to create a safe environment for the settlement and its gritty dwellers.

Ezra was a scholar by training and passion. As a scribe, he was a well-educated individual who had linkage to the priestly class. Proudly he could trace his genealogy to Hilkiah, the high priest during the reign of Josiah (see 2 Kings 22:4–20). His pedigree was unusually impressive since he could also claim Aaron in his ancestral lineage (see Ezra 7:5).

If Ezra had lived in New Testament times, he would have been known as a scribe—a teacher of the law. Some scholars believe that it was Ezra who compiled and wrote 1 and 2 Chronicles.

Indeed, he was a gifted scholar who was thoroughly familiar with Israel's history and who also had an opportunity to make history on his own as he led a band of settlers back to Palestine.

Ezra arrived at Jerusalem in August of 457 BC—after a four-month trip, with 8,000 new settlers. Immediately, he was confronted with a hot-bottom issue: concerns about a growing number of marriages between Jews and non-Jews. Such was the boiling arena unto which Ezra was thrust upon his arrival. Unbeknownst

---

[3]Most scholars believe that there is a relationship between Artaxerxes and Queen Esther, and the vast majority argue that Artaxerxes may have been Esther's stepson.

to them, however, he was the bearer of good news. The mighty king of Persia had entrusted him to:

> appoint magistrates and judges to administer justice to all the people of Trans-Euphrates—all who know the laws of your God. And you are to teach any who do not know them. Whoever does not obey the law of your God and the law of the king must surely be punished by death, banishment, confiscation of property, or imprisonment. (Ezra 7:25–26, NIV)

Ezra, though a priest, was commissioned with a wide array of authority. His role was to get the resettlement project on a fast track. By doing so, he would garner an honored place in the nation's history.

Nehemiah: Thirteen years later (444 BC), Nehemiah breaks onto Jerusalem's arid landscape. He is the third individual in our story who had a crucial role in the re-establishment of Jerusalem. Whereas Ezra was a scribe/priest, Nehemiah was a layperson. He emerges as the cupbearer to King Artaxerxes. A cupbearer was much more than simply someone who served the king his drinks. He was the food taster as well—a highly-trusted official who played a significant role in the life of any ruler. That individual risked his life for the monarch—literally, every day.

Consequently, it is understandable that a strong bond of trust would develop between a king and his cupbearer. The cupbearer likely followed the king from place to place, given the fact that he was a key person within the entourage. However, we meet Nehemiah in Susa, the winter capital of Persia. As with any zealous Jew of the era, the status of Jerusalem was uppermost on his mind. Thus, when some travelers arrived from Zion, Nehemiah grills them with questions regarding the general outlook of the enterprise. Sadly, there is no good news. The city continues to be beleaguered by its enemies and hampered by apathy from within. The work of reconstruction has halted, the walls are down, and the people are demoralized.

The report has a devastating impact on Nehemiah. His spirit is dampened, and he wept, mourned, and fasted. In his display of emotions, one detects the degree of attachment that he felt for the city. Most people in his place would not want to get involved. He was removed physically and could have easily theorized the entire Jerusalem episode as God's punishment. He could have ignored the facts and moved on. In his somber mood, he prays to God for direction. He wants to help his fellowmen. He decides he *will* get involved. He prayed and reflected for nearly four months. If we fast-forward to the actual time spent in rebuilding the walls, it was fifty-two days, which means he prayed more than the actual duration of the project.

Prior to that encounter, we have no information about Nehemiah. We can deduct that he was born in exile and had been a very successful public servant. As a devout Israelite, he is determined to do something for his brethren engaged in the task of rebuilding Zion. Notwithstanding the devastating report, he sets out to painstakingly work out the details for a possible mission to the city itself.

For four months, he garners information. The cupbearer explores every potential scenario for a possible trip to Jerusalem: construction costs, traveling details, permits, military protection, etc. It is praiseworthy to grasp the number of details that he garnered by way of due diligence.

Four months later, God opens a door for Nehemiah to state his case before the monarch (see Neh. 2:1–8). Shrewdly, the king's trusted man and would-be rebuilder of Jerusalem couches his request in a sentimental note: he wanted to go to the land of his ancestors and honor their memory. There is a subtle insinuation that their sepulchers may be in disrepair.

By presenting his case persuasively to the king, he is granted a leave of absence. He was also given the necessary documentation that he needed so as to assure the proper collaboration from royal officers. It was further clarified that he was going as a governor and to build the walls and gates of Jerusalem.

The day that Nehemiah dismounted his mount, he was an unknown individual to the settlers of and around Jerusalem. However, that was soon to change. Without wanting to draw much attention to himself, he secretly scouted the walls and assessed the damage and the repairs needed. When he knew fairly well what needed to be done and how to go about it—he called for a general assembly.

Before the local leadership, he challenges them that it is time for the walls to be rebuilt. Some of those assembled may have been skeptical and maybe even mused: *another dreamer who thinks this is going to be a walk in the park.* Yet, Nehemiah is able to persuade them and capitalize their goodwill. Once he had them on his side, the work progressed quickly. He divided the task into small stretches and gave responsibilities to individual families. The people responded.

Amidst gruesome opposition he is to build the wall in relatively quick time—fifty-two days. Following the completion of the walls, he organized a feast of celebration. Needless to say, the festival of thanksgiving was a spiritual watershed. Additionally, social disparities were addressed and remedied. The repatriates entered into a positive period characterized by optimism and progress. Nehemiah seems to have remained in Jerusalem for a number of years as governor and all the while being a moving force amongst the returnees.

Chapter 3
The Exile

B **abylon**: Babylon was an impressive city. Its greatest king, Nebuchadnezzar, had employed much of the royal treasury to make it uniquely so. There were canals that traversed it, and impressive temples were scattered throughout the metropolis. Its citizenry enjoyed spacious boulevards that were magnificent works of urban planning. As the city that had mastered the entire Middle East, Babylon lived up to its many hyperboles. Indeed, it was known as Babylon the great (see Dan. 4:30).

A by-product of a polytheistic belief system is a multiplicity of deities. As such, multiple shrines were scattered within the capital. However, none was more beautiful than the one dedicated to Bel Marduk. Known as the Esagila, it was in the center of the city. It contained two large courts and the shrine itself. It was among the greatest architectural wonders of the city, a city well-known for its extravagant architecture.[4]

---

[4]C. Mervyn Maxwell, *God Cares*, 2 Vols: *The Message of Daniel for you and your Family* (Boise, Idaho: Pacific Press Publishing Association, 1981) Vol.1, 61.

Since Babylon was the political center of the greatest empire on earth, it was also beautified by lavish palaces. Among the most noteworthy were those of Nebuchadnezzar. The king of Babylon had three palaces built, each one superseding its predecessor in splendor. The capstone of his palaces was one that was roofed with trees and plants, known in history as the Hanging Gardens and often included among the Seven Wonders of the Ancient World.

The ruling class was composed of military men, priests, magistrates, princes, and concubines. That class lived in luxury that was evident in their opulent lifestyle. After all, it was this elite class who most benefited from the tribute that poured into the Babylonian coffers from distant conquered lands and peoples.

Additionally, Babylon was a secure city. Its massive walls would deter any conquest. The Euphrates River provided ample water supply, a vital necessity of any city. Therefore, it was well understood that to conquer Babylon by military assault was virtually impossible. It was into such a grand city that an initial wave of Jews was transported in 605 BC.

Captivity: Up until that time, captivity for the Jewish nation was unthinkable. Simply put, they considered themselves as Yahweh's *unique people*. Additionally, the land of Palestine had been promised to them, as they understood it, forever. The temple—site of God's holy manifestations—would not be left unprotected by God. It was His showplace for the entire world to see and learn of His character. Therefore, it was an unfathomable devastation to the prevailing mindset when, in the summer of 586 BC, the city was utterly plundered and destroyed. Furthermore, the temple was burned. It was inconceivable. The city lay in ruins, and God's people were exiled to a foreign land. They had been conquered, humiliated, and subjugated by an utterly pagan power.

Now, they longed for Zion! They felt so alien in that strange land: different in dress, language, food, and religion. Records exist of the sarcasm leveled at the Jews in the land of their captivity.

> By the rivers of Babylon we sat and wept when we remembered Zion. There on the poplars we hung our harps,

for there our captors asked us for songs, our tormentors demanded songs of joy; they said, "Sing us one of the songs of Zion!" How can we sing the songs of the LORD while in a foreign land? (Ps. 137:1–4, NIV).

Spiritual Application

Eden: The human race was living in an exceedingly beautiful paradise—Eden. It would be theirs as long as they conformed with the Creator's leading. However, due to rebellion, they were banished from that bountiful land. Satan, the oncoming prince of the world, had enslaved them. They were no longer free. Their daily existence changed dramatically. The beauty of the land was replaced by thorns and thistles. There were death and discomfort all around them.

In a land where pain and anguish were unknown, now weeping and wailing prevailed. In their previous habitat, mankind had not experienced death, but now it was part of everyday life. In the happy, carefree days of Eden, they communed with their Creator on a personal level. Now, direct communication with the Lord had ceased. The joyous prior existence was marred by duress and labor. Oh, how Adam and Eve longed for those bygone days, living within God's will and in His assigned land.

Spiritual Captivity: Yes, because our forefathers divested themselves from God, today the Christian believer is captive in the land of the enemy. This world is not our home. We have lost our Eden home and now wander about waiting for our expected deliverance. Yet, for now, we must travail in this valley of fears and tears.

Life in the world is not amicable to the Christian. Our values and worldviews are in tension with those of the prevalent society. Its music is not our music. The songs of Babylon are in full opposition to the music of Zion. The songs of Babylon will squelch our desire for heaven. When feeding upon the vacuous songs of the world, its messages will mold us to the rebellious worldview they espouse. Hence, more reasons why we need to nourish our souls with the songs of Zion.

Songs of Zion: We need to constantly remind ourselves of the beauty of our future homeland and of the reward that await us. Yes—it is an awesome and unimaginable land that the Lord has prepared for His faithful saints. Understandably, the prince of this world is feverishly trying to distract us so that we misplace our focus, yet, we must not be deceived.

As believers, we should not allow our minds to be shaped by his raunchy views of love, marriage, and sex. Music has such an intoxicating force that it can change the course of an entire generation. The American scene of the 1960s is an example of it. Music and illicit drugs, for the most part, radicalized a passive generation. How true the words of Andrew Fletcher ring in our ears: "Let me write the songs of a nation, I don't care who writes its laws."[5]

On the other hand, gospel songs fill our minds with the values, hopes, and aspirations of the saints who penned them. They are the *hits* that have nurtured the church through ages past. Such compositions have brought many a wayfaring child back to the loving arms of a gracious Savior. Their words and melodies have uplifted many a saint weighed down by the cares of this world.

Visiting a dear saint whose earthly pilgrimage was coming to its end, I asked her which was her favorite gospel song. Without hesitation, she answered: *Más Allá del Sol* (*Far Beyond the Sun*).[6] When someone is facing the imminence of death, they seek out the time-tested and soul-soothing songs that have been the bulwark of the church for centuries. In that saint's case, it was a song that spoke about the heavenly home that awaited her. Let us then avail ourselves of such hymns to bolster our faith walk as we await the King of Kings.

At Home in Babylon: There is another lesson we can glean from the Babylonian captivity. As the years passed, the exile became

---

[5]Andrew Fletcher (1653–1716) was a Scottish politician and writer, and this quote is attributed to him.
[6]Emiliano Ponce (1889–1966) was a Mexican musician who was the director of the presidential musical band in Mexico from 1919–1922. When he became a Seventh-day Adventist he resigned and began to work for the church. He wrote and arranged *Más Allá del Sol*, which conveys the yearnings of the Christian believer as he awaits for a new home in heaven at the second coming of Jesus.

tolerable. Of course, they spoke about returning to Palestine, but it was more of a cliché than a conviction riveted in their hearts. Simply put, they were assimilating the Babylonian way of life. The earlier generation that had been driven out of Jerusalem was passing away, and it was being replaced by those born and raised in Babylon. For them, talk of returning to Jerusalem was mere lip-service. They could not embrace the desire to go back to a place for which they had little emotional connection.

Gradually, some of the Jews became entrenched in Babylonian society. They acquired businesses and experienced a good life. Daily they dealt with Babylonians who were not all that different from themselves. Thus, a certain degree of acculturation took place. For those who were achieving social mobility, there was not a burning passion to go back to the rubble of the city of their ancestors. For them, Babylon had become *home,* and they were quick to remind themselves of the prophet's admonition (see Jer. 29:5–7).

> *The earlier generation that had been driven out of Jerusalem was passing away, and it was being replaced by those born and raised in Babylon. For them, talk of returning to Jerusalem was mere lip-service. They could not embrace the desire to go back to a place for which they had little emotional connection.*

However, there was a small group—a remnant—who longed to go back to Canaan. Babylon *was not* their home. As much as they had lived there and had spent decades there—their hearts were still attuned to the "glorious land."[7] Nevertheless, the idea of returning to Palestine was one that only God could maneuver

---

[7] Daniel had reached the upper echelon of Babylonian society; had achieved incredible success in Babylon, yet for him, the only "glorious land" was Palestine (see Dan. 11:16, 11:41), for it was the land that God had promised to Israel. For Daniel, Babylon was simply the place where he lived while yearning for the "glorious land."

and orchestrate. On the surface, the Jews were like any other population group which had been conquered and scattered within the empire. However, there was something that the children of Israel possessed which no other group was privileged to have.

The Word of God: The Jews had the scrolls of the prophets, which, in turn, contained the conditions under which the Lord would bless and shield them. Such manuscripts were studied and analyzed to glean a "word from the Lord." Through diligent research they were able to unlock timely prophetic pronouncements. Thus, the books of Isaiah and Jeremiah were very relevant in their search for "present truth."

As a high officer in the government of Babylon, one can safely assume that Daniel lived well and had all of the comforts of life at his disposal. However, though he had spent the bulk of his life in Babylon, emotionally and spiritually, he identified with his fellow exiled kinsmen. His devotion to the land of his birth was such that, habitually, he would pray facing Jerusalem.

Daniel's diligence was rewarded by coming across portions of Jeremiah, which in no uncertain terms, predicted the duration of the exile—seventy years (see Jer. 25:12). Such prophetic utterances placed the captivity in perspective and gave them the needed stamina to survive the hardships of their confinement. Furthermore, it provided a time-frame so as to know when the end of their travail could be anticipated.

Similarly, for believers today, we need to listen for a "word from the Lord." History is moving toward its final glorious climax, and we need to have a sense of where we are in the flow of prophecy. Yes, the church needs to be mindful and watchful of what is taking place around it. The revelations that we may glean might just be heartwarming.

> Therefore keep watch for you do not know when the owner of the house will come back—whether in the evening, or at midnight, or when the rooster crows, or at dawn. If he comes suddenly, do not let him find you sleeping. What I say to you, I say to everyone: "Watch!" (Mark 13:35–37, NIV)

Final Liberation: We anticipate that one day soon, we, too, will be liberated. We have such a hope. In terms of its cosmic dimensions, it will be an awesome God-moment. Those who yearn to return to Canaan will be taken from this world to Heavenly Canaan. While we await and anticipate that day, let us not lose courage as we wobble in the land that yet holds us captive. One day soon, the liberty bell will ring, the trumpet will sound, and we will be set free. Prophecies will be fulfilled, and we will go home! I can hardly wait!

Chapter 4

A Remnant

L**ife Was Good**: The first Persian decree offering the Jews liberty to return to their homeland was issued in 537/536 BC. It was welcome news to the exiles. The exiles of the first wave by then had spent nearly seventy years in exile. Thousands of others were also brought to Babylon for security reasons and political fence-building in subsequent years (597 BC and 586 BC). Unquestionably, by the time of the decree many of them were in their middle or late years.

Hence, their children had been born in exile and had never set foot on the hills of Palestine. For them the Promised Land was an-oft repeated phrase that was dear to their forefathers. Yes—stories of going back was part and parcel of the exiles' mindset, and yet for many who had been born in exile, Jerusalem was only a lifeless proper noun of their recent past. Plainly put, many had been born in Babylon, and that was their primary point of reference.

Staying Behind: With that backdrop, it is not surprising that as the initial caravan trekked out of Susa in 536 BC, the vast majority of exiles chose to remain behind. Although nearly 50,000 were stirred into action and joined the first wave that returned—still, that was only a fraction of the potential count (see Ezra 2:64–65).[8] The zeal for the motherland of those staying behind was tame and well under control. Many were able to rationalize their decision to stay behind as being strategic. As successful businessmen and entrepreneurs who remained in Persia; they would become a pipeline in providing financial and logistical support for those who had departed. That was the rationale of some for remaining in the land of their captors.

For the entrepreneurial community, the proposition of going to the "desirable land," was not a desirable idea at all. They had businesses to run and families to steer. Their homes had luscious gardens and many amenities of a successful life. What about their children? Were the ruins of Jerusalem sufficient reason to risk the safety and future of their families? Many weighed all the options, and for many it was a logical response: "We'll stay."

In their efforts to make life in Babylon tolerable, the exiles came up with an alternative place for fellowship, teaching, and worship. The synagogue, a staple of Jewish life ever since, had its beginnings during the Babylonian captivity. It served the function that the temple had served for their forefathers in the land of Canaan—a central venue for fellowship and community. Thus, in a subtle way, it eased the urgent need of dashing out to Jerusalem to rebuild the temple.[9]

Going Home: Thus, in 536 BC, the initial contingent of returnees assembles from various parts of the empire. The time has come to initiate their homeward march. Though a small minority, they

---

[8]There is not an exact figure as to the number of Jews in exile, but the estimates range from 200,000 to 600,000. Thus, the 50,000 that did return represented a small minority.
[9]During the exile, there was a felt need to meet congregationally to observe the Sabbath and other feast days. Lacking the temple, a simple building would do. Thus, scholars agree that during the Babylonian/Persian exile, the synagogue emerged to meet the need of community, fellowship, and teaching. Their success in providing a sense of community, is evident in that they continued to be a central gathering place, even after the Second Temple was erected. Alfred Edersheim, *The Life and Times of Jesus the Messiah*. (McClean, VA.: Macdonald Publishing Company, 1883), 431–432.

took the bold step of crossing the desert and beginning life anew in Palestine. They were a remnant that was willing to abandon the comforts of Babylon/Persia and exchange them for the harsh extremes of life in Palestine. For them the choice was based on a simple logical conclusion—as much as they may own/possess and lavish in Babylon, it was still Babylon. They were Jews; their natural ancestral home was in Judea. Their stint in Babylon was only due to the careless rebellion of their forefathers. Consequently, they would never see themselves as Babylonians, for they were not Babylonians. For that group it was rather simple to disengage from the allurements of Babylon and think in terms of "going home."

The returning group closed shops and made ready for the long trip "home." Appropriate purchases of goods and foodstuffs were made, and the excitement reached a high plateau. Travel in the desert demanded the safety and the security of numbers. Animals of burden were secured and the preparation forged forward. When considered from any logistical angle, what lay ahead was a challenging odyssey, if not a ludicrous enterprise.

Family Strains: There were also filial strains among families. Not everyone within the same clan felt the call of going back "home" when Susa *was* home. Such divisions shattered family unity. "I don't understand why we have to go back there to worship God; we can worship Him here just as well," was a sentiment expressed by more than a few. Preoccupation concerning the well-being of their offspring was the chant of many of those who remained behind.

For the remnant that wanted to go back, there was a sense of history that neither Persia nor progress could suppress. Now that the door had been providentially opened, they were determined to walk right in. Whereas in Persia they were exiles, strangers, pilgrims, and outsiders, Palestine offered them the excitement of a new beginning; in a place rich in cultural, spiritual, and historical meaning.

Their cause became that of returning to Palestine and rebuilding Jerusalem. It was their ancient homeland, and emotionally and culturally, they identified with that land. For that reason, they were willing to risk all, invest all, and bank on the Almighty God of Abraham. Now they would follow in his footsteps from Babylon to Canaan (see Gen. 12:1–6; Acts 7:2–4).

Spiritual Application

Anemic Response: The pathetic response to the clarion call of going back to Palestine was lukewarm. The dream of an entire generation was at their grasp, and yet, the reply was timid and half-hearted. As has been pointed out above, it was among the more successful that the response was most anemic. That generation, born in exile and bred within the Babylonian/Persian culture, was not crying to go back to the Promised Land. In fact, we can surmise that they felt pretty well-acculturated and comfortable within the trappings of the Persian Empire.

Up until now, we have drawn some parallels between the "Second Exodus" Jews and the Christian Church. However, at this point, I would like to be a bit more intentional and address some of the observations to also include the faith community that I know best and to which I belong: the Seventh-day Adventist Church.

I sense that a similar spirit pesters Adventism today. The years of the pioneers are long gone; 1844 and 1888 seem distant in time and experience. As a people we have made significant inroads in many facets of life. Many among us have become polished and educated; our institutions have grown in stature and size. Perhaps because of our perceived earthly success, talk of the Promised Land is not as readily repeated amongst us as in yesteryear. There are other issues much more immediate that need to be addressed and mended. Whereas the bulk of the energy and passion of our forefathers was entirely devoted to advancement of the kingdom of God, today, there are other peripheral issues that demand and occupy our keenest minds. Much in resources and energies is readily spent in the maintenance of the institutional infrastructure. We have indeed become successful but at a price.[10]

---

[10] The conundrum facing the church (mission vs institutionalism) has been artfully discussed by George R. Knight. Here are a few choice quotations from said author: [The church] "...has so many [institutions] that her chief administrators spend a large and crucial bulk of their time attending board meetings and trying to solve the increasing insurmountable problems of these institutions in a rapidly shifting complex social system." "I fear that in

Some among the younger generation have seen the ambivalence amongst us and have concluded that there is no need for urgency. The unwritten message they perceive is that there is time to do what one desires to engage in as long as one does not stray too far from the fold. Those who have been raised in the church and thus have heard a goodly amount of preaching regarding the end-times are the most susceptible to that rationale.

During my initial days in the United States Army, I was pleasantly surprised that there were a good number of fellow Adventists in the unit. Yet, I soon observed that they were not devoted to live within the boundaries of basic Christianity. It seemed that they had never internalized their beliefs, and the newly-found freedom away from home exposed it. As a new believer, I was shocked and saddened. I could not figure it out. But, it was obvious that something was missing in the upbringing of those fine young men.

Transparent Lives: I assume that most of us want to hear Bible-based messages that address contemporary affairs in a relevant fashion. Half-hearted preaching that avoids the dominant issues of the day is negligence by the watchmen of Zion. However, when there is a clear "thus saith the Lord," such preaching will stir up the rank and file into positive action. And how we need for the church to be stirred into action! The church sorely needs a generation that is fully committed to go into the trenches and give the devil a fit and a fight. Each generation has the potential to be that Spirit-powered generation that will turn the pendulum. Heaven awaits in anticipation.

How can we foster the dynamics that will enable that to be? I believe that we need to become real and transparent in our lifestyle. Those with whom we engage need to see and sense that we are a people of transparency in words and deeds. Our post-modern society has often scolded the church for its mixed messages. Consequently, it behooves the church to live in such a way that

---

too many cases the church and its institutions have become a "jobs program" and that institutional survival has become an end in itself." "Good preaching, loving pastoring, and convincing evangelization are the greatest needs of Adventism today." George R. Knight, *The Fat Lady and the Kingdom: Adventist Mission Confronts the Challenges of Institutionalism and Secularization*. (Boise, ID: Pacific Press Publishing Association, 1995), 15–20, 52.

the unbelievers cannot deny the power of the gospel to transform individuals. That is the type of sermon that cannot be misquoted or ignored. In fact, it is the grandest of all sermons.

A dear friend of mine grew up in a typical Adventist home. It was normative in that household for the father to expect each child up for family devotions early in the morning. Needless to say, the children despised the early rise and seemingly unprofitable routine. One evening, as the young man was arriving home, a bit on the late side, he heard his father in his room praying. He stopped and listened and heard his dad claiming the promises of God for each one of his children, and with cracking voice, pleading with the Lord for their conversion. As my friend has shared with me, that experience changed his life. He came to the conclusion that his father's faith was legitimate and worth emulating.

Engagement: Our spiritual Adventist forerunners achieved incredible advances for the cause in a relatively short time. How were they able to accomplish so much in so little time? When one reads their sermons, diaries, and books, one detects that building up the church was paramount to them. They embraced that challenge full-heartedly and with full commitment. They knew not ambivalence nor short cuts. They knew their Bibles, and they knew their Lord. Thus, their contagious attitude impacted a whole generation of new believers, which was filling the church ranks in the second half of the nineteenth century.

One can only marvel at the massive missionary enterprise on which the church embarked in the late 1800s. It was all evidence of how well the pioneers had been able to inspire a new crop of believers. Their vision and zeal had been successfully passed on to the generation coming behind them. When the torch is not faithfully passed on to the next generation, we can only anticipate confusion and lackluster devotion. It is what happens when runners in a relay race pass the baton; it needs to be done precisely right.

> *When the torch is not faithfully passed on to the next generation, we can only anticipate confusion and lackluster devotion.*

If there is a misstep, it can lead to embarrassment and worse, loss and defeat.

Cultural Challenges: As we endeavor to apply the lessons of the returning exiles of 536 BC, one must take into account the fears that dwell within the human psyche. Not everyone is able to put spiritual enterprises above family affairs. Not everyone is a risktaker or a trailblazer. Most people would rather wait for the other fellow to take his chances, and if he fails or succeeds, then they know which way to go. Yet God expects us to be bold and tenacious. The Christian path, regardless of how rosy it is painted, is a rough road. Self-denial and self-sacrifice are its trademarks. The path to the heavenly Jerusalem is painstakingly difficult (see Acts 14:22).

Moreover, may we remind ourselves that the road to heaven is called the "narrow path." It is not a brisk walk in the park. On the contrary, it is a staggering journey beleaguered on all sides by foe and disgruntled family (see Matt. 10:36). Therefore, we have to make certain decisions as we initiate our journey. Even if we are not to be the heroes of history, we need to be bold and decisive in our actions. There is too much at stake. It is not a time to tinker; it is time to be on the offensive. Long enough have we marked time.

Obstacles and confrontations there will be. Jesus warned us about it (see John 16:33). It will be unavoidable as long as the church is what God wants it to be. The predominant North American culture is primarily entertainment-driven in its scope. If an activity lacks such qualities, it is typically cast aside and labeled as boring. Since Christianity is not by definition self-centered, its mere core principles clash with the prevalent culture, which is totally preoccupied with the individual. Yet, self-denial is the benchmark of our faith. While that is a trait that is typically admired, for the believer, it is often translated into being an oddball and a fanatic. Well, so be it!

Countercultural: For a society that is self-obsessed, Las Vegas is a valid symbol of that mindset. It is where hedonism is lived to the nth degree. Fun, sensuality, and frivolity are promoted and touted as the way we are to reward ourselves: work hard; play hard. Regardless of what the slick promos may say and imply, that lifestyle is shallow and only satisfies the carnal component of an individual, while its spiritual sphere is completely void of sense and direction. Yet, that is the prevailing philosophy that is projected to the entire world by the American media. For most of the world, American entertainment (movies, music, and television) is the staple diet in their entertainment. Consequently, one can visit almost any spot on the globe and be surrounded by American media and its overt promotion of self-gratification.

Yet, that is the world where today's church has to exist and flourish. It is a world that touts premarital sex and deviant sexuality and denies the existence of absolute truths. Nonetheless, the church cannot waver. It must be undaunted in order to impact society for good. In order to make a difference, we must be different. Ships are safe on the dock, but they were not made to be on the dock; rather in the open ocean battling the forces of nature. As heirs of the Reformation, we need to be unrelenting as we enunciate the outlandish shortcomings of contemporary values.

The church can be passive and become pointless, irrelevant, and noninfluential, or it can be bold and become an agent of societal change. That latter will carry some risks, and yet, it is the biblical pattern. The apostles were men "who turned the world upside down" (Acts 17:6, NKJV). Incidentally, such words were spoken by an outsider who was unsympathetic to the work of the church.

Apostolic Model: We look back with sentimental eyes to the apostolic church. Yet, it did have its problems and issues—quite a few, in fact. However, it was a bold church. It did not refrain from speaking out in the marketplace or in the workplace (Acts 5:41–42). Christians and their message were everywhere; they could not be avoided. Subtly, yet intentionally, the message of Christ was permeating the culture. Hence, the church became God's arm for massive societal change.

Being the remnant carries an awesome responsibility. In the case of the returning exiles, they needed to grasp the vision and get to work so that Jerusalem could be rebuilt. Once that would take place, the nation would surge as a viable entity to reveal God's character to the world. Though few in numbers, they took the challenge and set out through the desert to be used by God to accomplish the noble mission. The mission of today's remnant is not any less important. It has the role of working diligently so as to set up God's kingdom on earth. It is a sobering expectation and yet one for which we have been assured success (see Matt. 24:14).

Chapter 5

Crossing the Desert

A Long Way: Look at the map. The distance from Susa to Jerusalem was around 900 miles. Any way you look at it—embarking on such an undertaking was a demanding and dangerous enterprise. Unsurprisingly, portions of the landscape were extremely difficult, and these included long, meandering routes that limited real progress. Additionally, the travelers needed to be fully aware of where water and other amenities were to be found. Moreover, it was a sober and risky ordeal, for it was not uncommon for marauding thieves to attack small caravans and pillage their goods. Add to that the occasional sandstorms, which could blind and confuse the best of scouts. Extremities in temperature only added to the discomfort and challenges of such a long journey.

In the case of the returnees, the harsh conditions were made even more difficult by the potential futility of the enterprise. As the days wore on, their minds began to rehearse some of the pointed criticism that had been leveled at them during the preparation phase. Many friends had questioned the judgment of those embracing the challenge of going back to Palestine.

> Could it be that their friends were correct and they were wrong?
> What did the future truly hold for them?
> Was failure a possibility?

The Motivation: As the excited band of Jews began their historic trek toward Palestine, they found comfort by banding together. Their significant number provided a sense of success to the mission.[11] In spite of its huge composition, they marched forward. Theirs was one goal and one mission—to arrive at Jerusalem safely. Again, we must be reminded of their passion and motivation. The ultimate motivating factor for these individuals was that they were partaking in a mission that would dramatically affect the future of thousands of their brethren scattered throughout the empire. For such a mission they were willing to risk their lives by crossing a lifeless desert. It was that visionary component of their role that, above all else, made their journey tolerable.

Desert Crossing: To successfully cross a desert, there are some practical tips that should be observed. One of these is that one does not cross the desert alone—you join a caravan, a group, a band of fellow travelers. By doing that, you gain the benefits that an entire group offers. As part of a caravan, you will find comfort and safety in numbers. A desert is a very lonely and dangerous place, and you need the protection as well as the safety offered by a clan. Thus, the Jews did well in organizing themselves into a large band.

Water: Deserts do not offer much in the sphere of comfort and sustenance. The arid environment does not produce the nourishment needed for humans to survive its harsh climate. Therefore, uppermost in the list of *must-have-items* when traversing a desert is water. It is key for survival. The precious few oases along the

---

[11]In Ezra 2:64, we are given specific numbers as to the composition of the first wave of exiles that returned under the leadership of Zerubbabel. There were 42,360 free Jews who chose to return. In addition, there were 7,337 servants whom scholars believe to be Gentiles. All in all, it was a huge enterprise that set out to cross the 900 miles of distance between Susa and Jerusalem.

way would serve to replenish the dwindling supplies of "God's gift," as water was appreciatively termed. Without those areas of relief and rest, crossing a desert is practically impossible.

Caravan Guides: A caravan needs an experienced driver/guide. Such individuals know the desert—they can read weather patterns and forecast upcoming weather-related events. Guides would make the necessary decisions to seek and assure the safety of those under their charge. In the desert it is not unusual for sandstorms to break out with little prior warning. The treacherous weather patterns can and do change with unsuspected speed. That is why the role of the guide was vital to a successful desert crossing.

Mirages & Disorientation: The bareness of the desert terrain can play games with the mind and the senses. One such mind alteration is a mirage. These mind-altering experiences have wreaked havoc on desert travelers through the ages. Another pitfall of desert travel is the easiness with which an individual can become disoriented. Since the desert landscape does not exhibit major variations in its contour, it can easily confuse and deceive the traveler into wandering off-course. Once orientation has been lost, it is very difficult to regain it. Unchartered wandering in a desert can be catastrophic. Thus, there is a factor of life or death in keeping the path plotted out by the caravan guide.

Spiritual Application

The Calling: God is calling a people all around the world. The message is going forth, and large numbers of people in every part of the globe are coming forward to join God's remnant church. It is thrilling to hear about the waves of individuals who are daily taking a stand for the cause of Christ. Yet, it is not easy. In every culture, in every stratum of society, there is hostility—at times blatant and brutal. Yet, the people keep going to the cross—even at the risk of physical harm.

Why do these individuals risk their social standing within a community, willing to become pariahs and sustain the brunt of criticism and ostracism? The answer is the same one that has propelled truth-seekers throughout history. People are seeking answers; seeking a better life. Rich or poor, many have realized that their lives are still empty and void of true happiness. Christianity offers them a new beginning and a positive outlook on life. The follower of Jesus will view his country and culture differently. The body and its upkeep are also seen through new eyes. Social sensitivity, which is dormant in most of us, suddenly is awakened as one considers the plight of others less fortunate. Concern for the planet is heightened. That, in part, is what the gospel of Christ is doing for countless millions around the world.

Congregation: In traveling the desert, there was safety and support in numbers. It is likewise for believers. One needs to connect with a vibrant congregation and be part of it. There, the believer will find the guidance and nourishment that will sustain his experience. It is registered by the Holy Spirit that the Lord "added to their number daily those who were being saved" (Acts 2:47, NKJV). A vibrant church will provide a nurturing atmosphere for all to grow and fellowship. It should never be a hotbed of criticism and clashing egos. Rather, it is to be a fortress to protect and shelter the individual from external trials.

> *As we cross the spiritual deserts of this world, we must make sure that we are bringing along some nourishing food.*

On a number of occasions, individuals have accosted me and have articulated their lack of commitment to the church because "there are hypocrites in the church." To them I respond that it is true and that I have met my share of them. However, I will also share with such people that just as there are hypocrites in the church, there are also godly saints. Indeed, I have met many of such individuals in whose presence you sense holiness. Then the proposition is plain and simple: if one wants to grow and mature as a Christian, one will seek out those who are holy and righteous and mingle with them. By sitting at their feet and worshipping alongside of them, one will gain a better footing and walk on the "path of the righteous" (Prov. 4:18, NIV).

The Word: To cross a desert, a traveler needed an ample supply of food. Likewise, as we cross the spiritual deserts of this world, we must make sure that we are bringing along some nourishing food. The Word of God is such food. Let me remind you how Jeremiah expressed it: "When your words came, I ate them; they were my joy and my heart's delight" (Jer. 15:16, NIV). Finding a portion of our day to delve into the Word of God is not only wise counsel, it is necessary in light of the demands of the journey in which we are engaged. Nutritionally speaking, we are what we eat. Spiritually speaking, if we do not nourish ourselves from the Word, we become weak, and thus, the journey becomes laborious and a hardship. Consequently, we become an easy target for the enemy who is seeking those whom he can disorient away from the flock (see 1 Peter 5:8).

We must make it a point of internalizing the Word of God (see Ps. 119:11). As we memorize portions of the Word, it resides within us, and it is part of our spiritual quick response when assailed by the evil one. Our Lord modeled that for us when He was fiercely tempted in the wilderness. On that occasion, it was His principal weapon to fend off the tempter. Inversely, if we have not stocked our minds with the Word, then we have precious little to use in our spiritual arsenal. Remember that Satan, our ferocious adversary, will be constantly seeking ways to dampen our joy and accuse us of having no right to salvation. However, the many wonderful and reassuring promises found in the Bible can bolster any Christian under any circumstance. In its pages we are reminded that we are a child of God and that no one can pluck us out of His hands (see John 10:28).

Shepherds: The caravan leaders were people who thoroughly knew the desert and its many pitfalls. They understood the way of the desert and the best routes to take to avoid its many snares. In our present church setting, God has placed pastors and teachers who fulfill a similar role. The pastor is to be a leader of the flock. That is precisely what the word pastor means—a shepherd. As a shepherd, the pastor is to be acquainted with his members and love them. The apostle Paul had the heart of such a shepherd: he would cry and rejoice with them (see Rom. 12:15). There is to be full identity with the membership. Being there for their high and low points in life is one sure way of interweaving that relationship. When that is practiced, a sense of family emerges that bonds the pastor and his flock.[12]

A pastor is also to alert those under his watch from doctrinal deviancy that often creeps into the household of faith. These may include doctrinal derision from progressive/liberal teachers and/or ultra conservative mindsets as well as a host of other fads and fallacies that steal their way into congregations. One way of repelling such destructive forces is to maintain a fresh preaching and teaching ministry in which the Bible is expounded for the edification of the congregants. Thus, the pastor/teacher is a key individual in preparing the church for the assaults and trials faced during the spiritual desert crossing.

There is a noticeable need in the gospel vineyard for pastors who are visible during the week and heard with conviction from the pulpit on the Sabbath. The church needs such voices. It is recorded of Apollo that he was "powerful in the Scriptures" (Acts 18:24, MEV). Though every individual is gifted in his own area, being passionate about the gospel story is something that is expected of every minister of the Word (2 Tim. 4:2–4).

Additionally, the pastor is to be a watchman on the walls of Zion. Consequently, the minister needs to have a sense of the times, as did the sons of Issachar, "who understood the times and knew what Israel should do" (1 Chron. 12:32, NIV). In his prophetic role, the minister needs to be cognizant of the dominant issues of the day in light of Bible prophecy. That is a very significant role for the pastor. The leadership of Israel knew the prophetic message—for when pressed by Herod, they accurately stated that the Messiah was to be born in Bethlehem. Yet, they did not understand the times and

---

[12] Such harmony is wonderfully expressed in the classic gospel song, *Blest Be the Tie That Binds*;
   Blest be the tie that binds our hearts in Christian love;
   The fellowship of kindred minds is like to that above.
   Before our Father's throne, we pour our ardent prayers;
   Our fears, our hopes, our aims are one, our comforts and our cares.
   We share our mutual woes, our mutual burdens bear;
   And often for each other flows the sympathizing tear.
   When we asunder part, it gives us inward pain;
   But we shall still be joined in heart, and hope to meet again.

the seasons, for if they had, they would have also known that Mary's babe was none other than the promised Messiah.

Oases: As caravans moved through the desert, they would strive to arrive at the various oases located on their path. An oasis offered rest in a peaceful and safe environment. Additionally, it offered a change of scenery and a pleasant environment in which to refresh and refurbish. Time at the oasis was well-spent. Progress was evaluated, and modifications made where necessary. Amidst the unhurried and peaceful setting provided by the oasis, energy and goodwill were restored. Having rested, the caravan was ready to begin the journey anew. Needless to say, there would still be potential challenges along the path, but the time spent restoring the soul would pay off when confronting such difficulties. It would be so, for they had been restored.

As travelers on our way to the heavenly Jerusalem, we need to avail ourselves of strategic "oasis events." These can be weeks of spiritual emphasis, camp meetings, evangelism events, retreats, conferences, concerts, etc. The Christian walk is very demanding, and thus, we need to avail ourselves of such events to bolster our spiritual perception. Mingling and sharing with like-minded brothers and sisters is in itself an uplifting experience. At the end of the day, we will agree that such events served as a booster to nourish and to restore our souls. In fact, for some ailing saint, such events can be the jumpstart of a life that had lost its vision and focus. Hence, the spiritual traveler can richly benefit from such enriching oasis events.

Mirages: In times of dire stress, our minds play tricks on all of us. To the desert-weary traveler, it may project wonderful images of Edenic beauty lying just ahead. Soon the distortions are recognized for what they were: a deception of the mind, a mirage. Mirages are optical illusions caused by atmospheric conditions aided by stress and anxiety. Plainly stated, the individual is deceived by his own senses. The fact that our senses are so deceived speaks to the overbearing impact of a mirage. Yet, soon enough, the wayfarer realizes that he is still enveloped within the harsh desert setting. After such treacherous jolts, the pilgrim must tread on until he reaches the true land of milk and honey.

A mirage well illustrates the enticement of temptations on our pilgrimage to the heavenly Canaan. The shrewd enemy will place attractive delights in front of us that will make us meander from our defined path to the Promised Land. Such enticing attractions speak to our sensual side. We will see its sheer beauty and be beckoned to it. Yet, it is meant to distract and divert. It is part of the master plan to lure us away from our mission and ultimate destination. At times it can take the form of *new light,* which by its mere definition, tends to ward off the *old* light. Whenever we are diverted from our sure path to our destiny, we are wasting precious time while taking the risk of not finding our way back. Hopefully, we will detect in due time that it is all a mirage—a mere illusion; a cruel and vain deception of reality. So, fellow travelers, beware even of your own senses, for they can deceive you. Let us purpose to boldly move forward by faith; and not be dissuaded by any distraction (see 2 Cor. 5:7).

Chapter 6

Challenges to the Construction

Arrival: The very first company of believers arrived in Jerusalem in the summer of 536 BC. They had crossed 900 miles of harsh desert landscape. The able leadership of Zerubbabel and Joshua had provided security during the four-month trip, undertaken at the hottest time of the year (see Ezra 7:8–9). After pacing desert sand for months, the long caravan arrived at its destination. Yes, they had arrived at what was left of the City of David. It was evident that war had ravaged the capital city, and the victorious army of Babylon had wrecked its walls.

Everything was in shambles. For those who remembered Zion, it was only a shadow of its former beauty. But what broke the heart of the pilgrims was the state of their beloved temple. It was in total ruins—the House of Yahweh was not. Grass and weeds were growing within its various crevices. The ghostly spectacle shook them to the core. Few had imagined the city to be so devastated, which, in turn, shook their collective consciousness. In light of the gruesome sight, a number of them wondered whether they had made the proper decision in embracing the mission of rebuilding Zion.

Home at Last: Some, however, saw a glimmer of hope. They were home. Among the elderly, there were a few who remembered the city in its pre-exilic days. Sweet memories of the temple and its majesty were shared with the younger crowd. All recognized that their ancestors had dishonored Yahweh, and thus, the fires of the exile had been lit—but now the sons and daughters of that generation were given the privilege of erecting the temple anew.

Among that first wave of settlers, the vast majority had been born in exile. For them there was no memory of the former city. In fact, it was their very first excursion into Palestine. Yet, that generation welcomed the role that history had bestowed upon them. They were pleased to be given a chance to rebuild that glorious city of their forefathers. It was a monumental task, but they cherished the opportunity to accomplish a mighty deed for their Lord.

Winter Preparations: The first few months found the repatriates occupying themselves in erecting the basic mechanisms to survive in the new harsh land. These included dwellings, food supplies, shelter, and protection. As soon as those initial needs were met, they set about to work on the temple.

The very first portion to be erected was a makeshift altar of sacrifice so that sacrifices could be offered henceforth. By early fall, the feast of booths was observed, and its celebration added to the festive mood. The service was held, and the plans for the temple and city were shared with those in attendance. Because winter was setting in, the work in earnest on the temple site would be delayed till the spring of 535 BC (see Ezra 3:1–7).

During the rainy season, contacts were made with Phoenician coastal cities to supply and ship the necessary lumber. It was reminiscent of what Solomon had done in building his monumental temple (see 1 Kings 5). The task at hand was so glorious that it spread harmony and joy amongst the settlers. Indeed, there was a prevalent mood of optimism during the rainy and cold winter season.

Construction Begins: When spring made its appearance, the exiles were more than ready to begin the temple reconstruction. Excitement swelled up as arrangements were made to begin the task. There was a moving ceremony with the participation of priests, Levites, and musicians. It was indeed a very significant time—the initiation of the temple project had begun. Given how bleak such an event had seemed just a few years earlier, it was indeed a moment to celebrate and acknowledge Yahweh's leading in the turn of events. Songs and praises expressed the mood of the historical occasion.

However, amidst the joyful expressions, there was perceived wailing and lamentation. While some were crying with joy, others were indeed *crying*. Who were they? As it turned out, it was the older folks who had actually seen Solomon's temple in its full splendor. Their emotions betrayed them. They felt that God was dishonored by the seemingly small and simple structure that was to be erected. In place of their magnificent house of worship, they would have to be content with a mere semblance of the former one.

Construction Halted: One may perceive that their cry was an expression of reproach and self-condemnation. Perhaps the event in itself reminded them that it was their generation that had failed God. As we can imagine, the wailing put a negative spin on the groundbreaking ceremonies. The work stopped. A period of remorse and soul-searching set-in (see Ezra 3:8–13).

Additionally, when the people of the land realized that the Jews had come to rebuild and permanently settle Jerusalem, they were mightily upset. Quickly, they sought ways to impede the project. As part of their ploy, the Samaritans offered to help in the reconstruction. Their scheme was to get in on the inside and thus foster discontentment and dissension from within (see Ezra 4:1–3).

However, Zerubbabel and Joshua firmly declined their offer. That infuriated the Samaritans. In retaliation they sent letters to Susa in which they denounced the Jews and the project in the worst possible manner. These developments muddled the proceedings and led to a stalemate in the construction. Thus, the building project came to a complete halt (see Ezra 4: 4–24).

Construction Deferred: Weighed down by these events and the necessity of providing for their own families, many of the would-be temple builders changed course. The task of building their own homes became their primary interest. That is how things stood in the spring of 535 BC. For the next fifteen years, the temple project was not. It had fizzled. There was plenty of building activity—but it involved building and enlarging private dwellings. Sadly, the impetus that had brought them to Palestine gradually waned. In its place, life had taken on a monotonous and predictable pace for the would-be temple builders.

> *The impetus that had brought them to Palestine gradually waned. In its place, life had taken on a monotonous and predictable pace for the would-be temple builders.*

Prophetic Voices: It was then that God raised two prophets. The first of these was Haggai, and he appears on the scene in the year 520 BC. His powerful message had one goal in mind: to stir up the passive Jews into action and begin anew the reconstruction. Haggai gave himself entirely to that task and quickly refocused the mindset and jump-started the settlers into action. His short but efficient ministry had the desired effect: leadership and the people once again found passion and energy to rebuild the temple.

Zechariah, who followed him chronologically in 520 BC, was also adamant in his appeal for the temple to be restored. The tenor of his message, however, was aimed at Zerubbabel and Joshua, the political and spiritual leaders of the enterprise. Once he had their attention, the people followed, and progress moved rapidly. With Haggai's and Zechariah's admonitions and encouragement, the project picked up speed and moved forward at a fast-pace.

Spiritual Application

One Foundation: One lesson that one can glean from the narrative is that the settlers did not have to start from scratch. The general pattern of the city was still visible in spite of the fallen wall and debris. There were also remains of the temple building, indicating its layout and distribution. Therefore, their mission was to rebuild the house of the Lord in the very place where the other had previously existed. The new would be built upon the old model.

Likewise, we are called to build up the church of Christ on a worldwide scale. As much as it is a daunting task, we can be heartened by the fact that we need not reinvent the church. There is already a foundation on which to build. It is the foundation laid down by the prophets and the apostles. All we need to do is to follow in their footsteps (see Eph. 2:20).

Thus, there is no need for eccentric doctrines and/or new theologies. We already have the foundation and the cornerstone. Given that we have that crucial and vital component—foundation and cornerstone—we would do well to simply walk and work in the faith "once delivered to the saints" (Jude 3).

Obviously, the chief cornerstone is the Lord Jesus himself. He is irreplaceable. None other will ever hold, sustain, and lead the church through its final chapters. Therefore, the true church will be built upon the faith and ministry of Jesus—just as the apostolic church was built upon the pure teachings of the Lord. When it is built upon that Rock, it will be able to withstand all fury from within and from without (see Matt. 7:24–25 and 1 Cor. 3:11).

Internal Strife: The older generation was quick to react when they beheld the new structure; they cried, wailed, and spoiled it for the builders. In their minds, it was nothing like the previous edifice. Unwittingly, their reaction had an immediate negative impact upon the rest. A feeling of uncertainty and discouragement set in. Like a tremor, it shook the very core of their *raison d'ĕtre*. Similar to a groundswell, it spread, and soon, even leadership was discouraged. Yes, careless words and actions destroyed and disabled with tsunami-like effects.

A year earlier, these folks were still in captivity on foreign soil. By way of miraculous interventions, God had worked out their freedom from the mighty grip of the Persian Empire. Now they were in Palestine and poised to be part of a memorable event. They would have the privilege of erecting the temple and rebuild

Jerusalem. Yet, such a unique moment had been derailed. It was no time to cry; it was time to celebrate. The criticism put forth cooled off the enthusiasm of a historic occasion. It was a unique moment, yet the reckless and insensitive criticism by some from within soured the sweet moment.

It is even so today. Every time that God's people are about to launch into some enterprise that is going to bring honor and glory to God, the enemy trembles and seeks to find ways to derail it. One of his most effective ploys is to work from within—internal criticism and strife. One can easier take the criticism from those of the loyal opposition—sworn enemies on the outside—than from those on your team. It is much more difficult to digest because they are your colleagues, your own cheerleaders.

External Opposition: Needless to say, the enemy has numerous ploys to use against God's people. As viewed above, he uses internal strife to destroy fellowship and camaraderie. When that is not sufficient to bring down the project, he raises opposition from without (see Ezra 4:1). Those on the outside are the sworn enemies of God's people. They are out to destroy, if at all possible, the cause of God. And that is precisely what we find in the fourth chapter of Ezra.

The Samaritans felt rejected, and quickly, their "friendship" turned into vile opposition toward God's people. The very same people who wanted to come along and "help" build the temple now are vehemently opposed to the very same project. Their reaction made transparent their true intentions. Because they are not able to physically halt the operation, they turn to the state. One way or another, the work that is being raised by the Sabbath-keeping Jews needs to be crippled. They will hold no punches; they want the project disabled, and they will use their political clout to achieve that.

The church of God will continue to face similar wrath as it is building spiritual Jerusalem. Since we are not of the world, the enemies of God will continue to deter and derail. When simple arguments are properly answered and logically rejected, the enemies reveal their true character by seeking alliance with the *status quo*. Yet, by doing so, they admit a degree of frustration and defeat. So, it will be in the prophetic future. The mighty arm of government will be called upon to squelch the voices of those building up the church (see Rev. 13).

End-Time Scenario: Revelation tells us that such will be the strategy used by our enemies to ultimately accomplish what they are not able to achieve by other means. Just as our spiritual forefathers did not yield to the pressure and attacks heaped upon them by the surrounding peoples, neither should we. We should never compromise as we do what is right in the eyes of God (see Acts 5:29). Our goal should be to please Him above all else. Biblical and church history contain sufficient evidence for us to realize that when one stands for God, He will stand with His people. Needless to say, our truest enemy is Satan. He employs all of his sophistry to deter or derail the advancing church of Christ. Through an array of schemes and methods, his aim is the same: to halt the cause of God.

Progress: In spite of all the efforts put forth by the enemy, the Jerusalem building project eventually moved forward. In a document written by a Persian official, who was an eye-witness to the project, he relates to King Darius the visible progress. The officer states that the task was moving ahead with "diligence" and making "rapid progress" (Ezra 5:8, NIV).

So, it is today!

Every day around the world, an army of workers is building up Jerusalem—the church of Jesus Christ. It is being accomplished through sacrificial living and giving. Daily, thousands are taking their stand for Christ and His church. Thus, the temple of God is making "rapid progress" in our day as well. Neither communism nor capitalism has been able to halt its forward march. As we notice the church forging its way forward toward the kingdom, we must remind ourselves that it is doing so in spite of our frailties. It is because Christ is the true head of this enterprise called church. Indeed,

> The church has one foundation,
> 'Tis Jesus Christ her Lord;
> She is His new creation,

Through water by the word.
From heav'n He came and sought her
To be his holy bride;
With His own blood He bought her,
And for her life He died.

Chapter 7
Completion of the Temple

The newly-arrived settlers to the city of David had ambitious plans. The city would quickly be rebuilt, and life would once again thrive in their beloved Jerusalem. Their minds envisioned the happy choruses of children laughing and playing in its midst. But, as any Jew knew, Jerusalem would not be Jerusalem unless the temple was once again standing on the temple mound. So, uppermost in the minds of the newcomers was the daunting task of rebuilding the temple. In fact, it was the driving force behind much of what had compelled them to migrate.

However, after an emotional beginning and sour setback, the temple project had been tabled. The prevailing feeling was that it was not yet time for the Lord's house to be built (see Hag. 1:2). God desperately needed to jolt them into action. Thus, He engineered to bring onto the scene prophetic utterances. They would be God's mouthpieces, and they would inject vigor and vitality into the project. In the year 520 BC, two such individuals did just that.

Haggai: Haggai is an interesting prophet as his entire ministry lasted only seventeen weeks. His mission focused on reawakening the urgency of rebuilding the temple. Not much else is known about the prophet. Most likely, he came from Babylon and was living in the midst of the disheartened settlers. Consequently, it was easy for him to detect the lessening passion of the first wave of arrivals for the building project. As an on-site observer, it was fairly obvious to Haggai that the initial wave of enthusiasm had waned.

Consequently, God called Haggai to shatter the erroneous mindset that had taken hold of the leadership. Understandably, he was frustrated by the lack of action and the constant grumbling among the remnant. There was an urgent need to change the agenda and to do it quickly and dramatically. Undaunted, his messages were direct and bold. In essence he was saying—it *is* time to rebuild the temple. It was as if he was saying, "Brethren, leave your complacency, and grab your tools."

Timely Messages: During his brief ministry, Haggai shared five prophetic utterances with the community. The messages reached their hearts, and the people were reawakened into activity. The frazzled remnant arose, and with rekindled hearts, once again embraced their calling. The prophetic voice assured the settlers that God would be with them and that success would accompany their spiritual renaissance.

As the work progressed and the structure was taking shape, it became evident that the temple would be a far cry from Solomon's majestic temple. To allay any sense of failure and discouragement, the Lord gave Haggai a moving prophetic message. It was revealed to him that the Desire of the Ages, Messiah Himself, would walk in the midst of that simple and unimposing structure (see Hag. 2:7). To those hearing that revelation, it must have been extremely reassuring. To think that the long-awaited Holy One of Israel would honor the fruits of their labor! There was nothing more stimulating that could have been said. As the people internalized the wonderful message, their spirits soared.

In retrospect, one can say that the prophet had been very successful with his timely messages. He had aborted a disaster.

The malaise had been mended, and a new vision of the future had been cast before their very eyes. Having accomplished his mission, Haggai vanishes from the pages of Scripture. Nothing more is mentioned of this timely prophet who saved the day for the repatriated Jews.

Zechariah: As Haggai was wrapping up his meteoritic ministry, God raised yet another mouthpiece. His name was Zechariah. He enters the scene as the temple program is moving forward by way of Haggai's ministry. Whereas Haggai was exclusively concerned with the rebuilding of the temple, Zechariah's message was more far-reaching.

The revelations put forth by the prophet may be divided into two sections—the immediate and the eschatological. The first eight chapters stressed present conditions regarding the immediate task ahead. In those chapters he covered the stress, anxiety, and petty jealousies that such a project would birth. Yet, within that general framework, there are also messages of hope and encouragement for the leadership—Joshua and Zerubbabel (see Zech. 4:6–9).

The second part of the book (chapters 9–14) delves into the future of the nation and its eschatological role. Zechariah stresses that in the end times, the nations would form a coalition against Israel. However, Yahweh would fight for His people, and the enemies would be defeated and destroyed.

The triumphalist note at the end of the book was in itself of much encouragement. One can imagine how much encouragement such a message must have brought to the settlers. The building project had been delayed and demeaned due to the fact that many felt that the structure that they could build was not adequate for God. Yet, the ringing message of Zechariah is that the humble structure currently being built would play a major role in Israel's future history. In essence, they were made aware that they were building, not only for the present but for Israel's end-time role among the nations. It was thus understood that both Jerusalem and Israel would be major players in God's prophetic scheme at the end of the age.[13]

---

[13]Raymond B. Dillard and Tremper Longman III, *An Introduction to the Old Testament* (Grand Rapids, MI.: Zondervan, 1994), 427–436.

Thus, through the ministry of these two prophets, the building program was jumpstarted. The beleaguered settlers joined together and worked diligently. The malaise was gone. Additionally, the king of Persia fulfilled the royal decree by which the imperial treasury would cover the bulk of the construction expenses (see Ezra 6). The project was on a roll. Prophetic motivation, royal goodwill, and financial support paid off. By March of 515 BC, the temple project was completed!

Spiritual Application

Church Planting: Christ, as the head of the church, has specific instructions for His body of believers. He wants them to spread vigorously throughout the world. In some places there may be animosity and angst, and yet, the orders are to go to all nations (see Matt. 28:19–20). Neither poverty nor prosperity should deter the church from fulfilling its mission. You and I are to build up His church across the globe. But let me be clear about what the church is. The church that Christ wants us to build is more than mortar and wood; it is to be made up of spiritually-hungering individuals from all walks of life.

For the newly-arrived Israelites, there were many challenges: houses to be built, raising crops, and adapting to the challenges of a new environment. Yet even in the midst of it all, the Lord and the prophets placed upon them the burden of building up the temple. That speaks decisively of the high degree of expectation that Heaven places on the expansion of His spiritual kingdom. Chances are that we are not facing the life-threatening challenges that our spiritual forefathers faced. Therefore, it behooves us, even more, to step up and do our share of the work.

> Enlarge the place of your tent,
> stretch your tent curtains wide,
> do not hold back;
> lengthen your cords,
> strengthen your stakes (Isa. 54:2, NIV).

Research and real-life experience attest to a reality: planting a church is another form of evangelism. The consensus among church growth experts is that it is one of the fastest ways to spread the gospel and experience church growth.[14] Additionally, it is tapping into the talent pool of individuals who are normally passive in our congregations.

A number of years back, my associate pastor and I led out in a church plant in Tucson, Arizona. As we promoted the project and sought out volunteers to be part of the core group that would leave the mother church, we were pleasantly surprised. Some of those that stepped up were individuals whose faith lay dormant for years. Yet, they embraced the occasion to make a difference. The project infused them with a resurgence of faith and action. Indeed, to our delight, their spiritual life experienced a renaissance.

Opposition: As the people of God arose to build the temple, enemies emerged. The potential enemies had been there all the time but did not feel a need to oppose the people, for they were not doing anything to kindle their ire. Nevertheless, as soon as they saw the edifice taking form, the opposition consolidated. They moved quickly since their sole mission was to bring about discouragement and create havoc among the builders.

It is likewise today. Whenever individuals attempt to do something meaningful for the cause of God—enemies emerge. People

---

[14]Research has revealed that nearly all churches eventually reach a plateau in their growth. When that occurs, it is highly unlikely that it will ever exceed that plateau. Rather than trying to change the culture of a congregation that has topped off, a more exciting adventure is to start a new church. Peter Wagner, church planting guru, states it in unmistakable language: "The single most effective evangelistic method under heaven is planting new churches." Church plants in Adventism have confirmed Wagner's statement; "New Adventist churches grow at ten times the rate of established churches." The gospel commission assumes new churches emerging as the gospel was to be preached. Ron Gladden, *Plant the Future: So Many Churches! Why Plant More?* (Nampa, ID.: Pacific Press Publishing Association, 2000), 28, 41, 35.

who did not care much about your lifestyle when you were pursuing worldly pleasures now become concerned over your decisions. Passion for Christ is seen and labeled as suspect. Friends move to place the brakes on your zeal and have you slow down. But we need not fret—they are simply speaking for another lord—the lord of this world.

In spite of the enemies and distractions that they may hurl, the church is being built today by courageous and unselfish individuals. It is happening at a mind-boggling pace. People across the planet are joining the movement by the minute. Yes, literally by the minute. Jerusalem is being built!

By whom is God's church being built today?

- By the student missionary in Micronesia who conducts a VBS and teaches English ...
- By the retired couple who donate a year of their tranquility to be involved in teaching English and other skills in a secondary school in Korea ...
- By the cadres of ADRA personnel who donate their expertise to provide safe drinking water to an entire village in a land-locked country of Africa ...
- By the thousands of lay preachers who conduct countless Bible studies and cottage meetings in their neighborhoods, towns, and cities ...
- It is being built by way of the sacrificial donations that people around the world provide to foster mission expansion ...
- It is being built and sustained by the pastoral force across the world field ...

It is no wonder that the enemy is upset because the church of God is being built rapidly. As the church expands its sphere of influence, its mission will meet greater success and more opposition. Yes, the church is fulfilling Isaiah's vision of becoming a house of prayer for all nations (see Isa. 56:7). Our mission field is the world, and our task is to carry God's last-hour message to every corner of the planet. It is happening in our day and right before our very eyes. Are *you* part of it?

Chapter 8

Building the Walls

The biblical narrative is totally silent regarding the decades following the completion of the temple. One can surmise that the emotional high of rededicating the temple slowly and gradually subsided. Eventually, life became routine and uneventful. Perhaps unintentionally, but gradually, the focus was placed back on their personal needs. Survival in the new environment was still an ongoing challenge.

The next major event registered in the account takes place fifty-eight years later, and it is the arrival of Ezra and his contingent of settlers. It would be beneficial at this time to go back to chapter 2 (Personalities of the Second Exodus) to get reacquainted with Ezra and Nehemiah, the two outstanding personalities of the period. Suffice to say that Ezra was a Levite who was trained as a scribe, while Nehemiah was an official at the court of the Persian king, Artaxerxes (465–423 BC). They were strikingly different, and yet those would be the two individuals whom God would use in completing the rebuilding of Jerusalem.

Ezra's Arrival: Seemingly, the spiritual downturn in which the inhabitants found themselves was one of the issues that spurned Ezra into action in the year 457 BC. The fifty-eight years that had elapsed from the completion of the temple (515 BC) had shown that being back in Palestine did not automatically equate to spiritual growth. Because of their lackadaisical attitude, marriages between Jews and their pagan neighbors were a common occurrence. Therefore, no sooner had the scholar/priest arrived than he was asked to step in and try to halt that drift (see Ezra 9).

Walls Missing: The spiritual decline was also manifested in the precarious condition of the city walls, which had not yet been rebuilt. Consequently, Jerusalem lay quite vulnerable to enemy attack. Now that the temple had been rebuilt, which amounted to telling the pagan neighbors that they were there to stay, it was vitally crucial that the walls be quickly erected. Nothing would be safe in the city if it lacked walls. It was an obvious and urgent need. Yet, a leader was needed to move upon that project and see it to completion.

Nehemiah's Arrival: In distant Susa, one of the capitals of the Persian Empire, God moved to hand-pick the individual who would build the walls of Zion.[15] The man chosen was Nehemiah, the king's cupbearer. Nehemiah responded affirmatively and sought and obtained permission from the king to travel to Jerusalem. By 444 BC, he arrives in Palestine and immediately sets upon the task at hand. Within days, he has called a leadership council and lays before them the need for an all-out effort to raise the walls (see Neh. chapters 1 and 2).

His leadership style was visibly demonstrated in the detailed fashion in which he set about to reconstruct the walls. The entire project was divided into forty work sites. Each site was rebuilt by a small contingent of families who worked within their immediate dwelling area. It was a shrewd psychological move, for they worked with the understanding that they were securing their own

---

[15] The Persian Empire had three cities that served as capitals. Babylon, because of its majesty and illustrious history, was retained as an honorary capital, whereas Ecbatana, a city in Persia, served as a summer capital. Susa, a city in the Elamite portion of the Persian Empire, also served as a capital. The events described in the books of Ezra, Nehemiah, and Esther all mention Susa as the seat of government.

immediate environ. It was the equivalent of working for the safety of your home and family on a neighborhood watch. All were urged to work on the project. There were chores for everyone. One motivational factor was that by building the walls, *all* would be secured by the protection provided by the fortified walls.

Erecting the Walls: Nehemiah also sought the aid of those living on the outskirts of Jerusalem. Many responded to the appeal. The inhabitants of the nearby villages were a valuable surplus of labor to the already physically-taxed dwellers of the city. It was well understood by them that it would be to everyone's best interest to have a well-fortified city to which they could flee in case of prevailing danger. Jerusalem, with its walls built, would be such a place.

Since Nehemiah wanted the project completed in quick fashion, he urged all hands on deck, and nearly everyone complied. Among those giving their support were the movers and shakers of the region. The priests responded and worked on assigned portions of the wall. Even Eliashib, the high priest, was one of those who gladly lent his support and influence to the project. Businesspeople (perfumers, goldsmiths, and silversmiths) also responded and engaged themselves with the task. Women likewise responded and worked alongside the men. Needless to say, the cross-section of involvement at the work stations had an energizing effect upon the entire population.

Slackers: However, as it usually happens in such enterprises, not all who could have helped engaged in the project. For whatever reason, there were some who did not respond to the general appeal. History has provided us with the names of some folks who simply ignored the call. One such group were the nobles of Tecoa, who did not see fit to cooperate with the enterprise. Although they did not engage in the project, neither did they stand in the way of those who wanted to help. They simply did not believe in the project and, as a result, did not lend a hand. Perhaps others were not fond of the harsh working conditions and the demands that physical labor placed upon them. Although they were to enjoy the many benefits that a safe and secured city would furnish upon its inhabitants, they did not want to engage in the labor necessary to make it so (see Neh. 3).

Proactive Measures: On the other hand, there were declared enemies who proactively and intentionally harassed and threatened the working crews. Those enemies wanted to bring the project to a standstill. However, Nehemiah, the perceptive leader that he was, realized that proactive action was needed to assure the safety of the work crews. That led to the enactment of the following measure: workers were encouraged to bring their weapons to the job sites so that they could protect themselves in case of open hostilities (see Neh. 4).

Success: The project was staggering in its scope. Yet, the resilient leadership of Nehemiah shone time after time. Though distracted, harassed, and threatened, he did not bend. As a result, others were motivated by his no-nonsense style of leadership that made possible the completion of the project. In fact, it was completed in record time—fifty-two days. Yes, the walls that had been destroyed 142 years earlier were completed under the focused leadership of Nehemiah.

Spiritual Application

Whenever God's people venture into an area where the prince of darkness has had a stronghold, opposition will arise. At times it can surface from well-intentioned individuals who simply have an honest disagreement. Many times, it is those who will benefit the most by the gospel that rise up in opposition. They become defensive of the old ways and of what they have been traditionally taught. Sadly enough, it can also be based on petty jealousies, which the enemy magnifies so as to embroil and confuse the bigger picture. Either way, such antics detract and deviate from the main mission: to build up the church of God.

Prayer and Action: Nehemiah was a man of prayer but also a man of action. That he was a man of prayer is amply demonstrated by his numerous prayers sprinkled throughout his book. Yet, he did more than pray. His prayers were followed by action. By combining prayer and action, one has a dynamic combination that can realistically change lives and circumstances. He certainly practiced the maxim: *pray as if everything depends on God; work as* *if everything depends on you.* That is a powerful combination that breeds success and blessings. The congregation that wants to do mighty deeds for God today needs to embrace both of those components. It needs to pray for heavenly direction, and it needs to move and advance in response to those indications.

Vigilance: As Nehemiah analyzed the threat to the laborers, he set up a watch that was to be vigilant and attentive. Constant vigilance is a concept that needs to be ingrained in all of us. The church is the object of God's supreme love. Consequently, it can expect brutal and debilitating attacks. It is the aim of the enemy to incapacitate and sever her connection from the Lord. As a shrewd enemy, he does not slumber but is in constant flow, seeking out ways to halt the progress of God's movement.

In spite of being constantly harassed by the enemy, the people worked at the walls joyously. They understood that they were building something bigger than themselves. Likewise, we should find satisfaction in being part of something which is unique, relevant, and making a difference. One can sacrifice in many areas—time, energy, finances, etc.—when one identifies with a worthwhile cause. The church is such an institution. It has a transformative message for every human being on the face of the planet. Its teachings can uplift the downtrodden and bring hope to the hopeless. The values it shares are the core values that have welded civilizations throughout history. The church has survived the wrath of its enemies for millennia. It is bigger than nations, and it will outlast present civilization. That is a reality that should bolster us by its implications.

Labor of Love: Those who worked on the walls of Jerusalem devoted endless time and energy. They were not coerced or obligated to do so. They were volunteers. It was a labor of love. As we have seen, their composition was a cross-section of Jewish society. As volunteers, whatever contribution they made, it was done out of commitment to the Zion they loved. That was the glue that welded them together in spite of the danger, extreme weather, and personal sacrifice. Their main objective was to see the glorious city rebuilt for the sake of Yahweh and their personal safety.

Similarly, the church is an institution which is primarily maintained by volunteers. Upon close scrutiny, it is breathtaking the amount of ministry that takes place in the world-wide church, and that is carried out primarily by volunteers. We do not thank them enough. Yet, they do it year-in and year-out as a labor of love toward the Lord of the vineyard.

Separation and Protection: The completed walls would provide dual benefits for the city. They would shelter those within from potential enemies on the outside and would also serve to keep away those who were considered dangerous to the internal safety of the city. As the salt of the earth, the church is to impact its surrounding society, rather than the other way around. The norms and standards found within the Bible are to be defining landmarks, which in turn are to safeguard the believers. When the church upholds such standards, it will keep at bay the secular influence that seeks to permeate the faith community. May the wall provided by such norms and standards be an ever and constant source of separation and protection between God's church and the militant anti-Christian culture.

As the salt of the earth, the church is to impact its surrounding society, rather than the other way around.

Family: Families are the building blocks of the church. Therefore, the family is of extreme value to the body of Christ. Nevertheless, today's pleasure-absorbed society is not pleased when the church grows and thrives. Its mere presence annoys the existentialist who lives to please self. It is no secret that the family unit is under attack in modern society. The frontal attack began in the 1960s when marriage was seen as a throwback to a patriarchal era that employed marriage to exploit women.

With each passing decade, the attacks on marriage have emboldened. Hollywood typically portrays marriage in a non-ingratiating fashion. Unsurprisingly, there has been an erosion of respect for the marriage institution. The anti-marriage coalition is relentless. In the recent past, we have had the implementation of same-sex marriage to top it off. Tragically, many politicians, in order to appear as open-minded, caved in and supported such aberration.

Defend Marriage: The church, on the other hand, is to be the defender of the institution of marriage. It must define it, elevate it, and model it for the secular mindset of the twenty-first century. Because of the impact of the media and its lackluster portrayal of marriage, the Christian community needs to elevate it to its original stature of being "very good" (see Gen. 1:27–31, NIV). A few years ago, I was rudely made aware of how much the marriage institution has eroded. A leader within my congregation, and a man in his seventies, approached me and stated that he wanted to file for divorce from the wife of his youth. This was an individual who had served the church for years and in a number of relevant positions.

As a people, we have been blessed with special counsel and light in the area of marriage. We have in our midst material that is among the best there is. I remember reading such fine books during my teen years. As I read them, I was filled with awe for the marriage vow, and a deeply-rooted regard for the institution developed within me. In large measure, it was due to the laudable fashion in which the topic was presented in the church-produced material. Upon some reflection, I realize that if I had not been buoyed in my thinking by the literature that my church produced, I would have merely reflected and mimicked the prevailing anti-marriage view of the dominant society. And for that, I thank my church—the world body and my local congregation—for the wealth of wisdom that was made available to equip and educate its young people.

Nevertheless, I have a concern. I sense that today's generation is not being molded and equipped by similar guidance. Perhaps I say what I say due to the embarrassing number of failed marriages that I have witnessed in my ministry. Tragically, although fine material is still readily available, it is not being maximized by those needing it most.

Walls: We need to establish walls around our families just as the Lord placed a hedge around Jerusalem (see Ps. 125:1). Their safety and well-being should be foremost in our thinking and planning. Let us consider some of the hedges that we can construct around our families in our effort to shelter them from the ills of the world.

Clear, Rational Thinking: One wall which we need to erect for the spiritual survival of our children is to teach them to think for themselves. The prevalent culture is ever so intent on producing a generation that dresses, thinks, and acts alike. As that collective mindset emerges, conceived primarily by the entertainment industry, it is very difficult to depart from its herd mentality. Its tentacles are so embracing that many are willing to sacrifice values in order to find acceptance within. Whenever we can instill in our youth the ability to think clearly and rationally, we have done well. However, that is only half of the challenge.

Standing Up: The other half of the equation is to have them embrace the concept of boldly standing up for what they believe. We do not want to produce clones of the Pillsbury boy who is cuddly but has no spine. So, in addition to thinking for themselves, they will need to have the courage to stand for the convictions of their hearts. Being a Christian in a hostile setting is a tough proposition. Believers will be constantly challenged—from the playground to the board room—and they need to have a clear sense of who they are and its implications. The oft-repeated line is quite true: He who does not stand for something will fall for anything.

I have often heard testimonials where young people speak of wandering around aimlessly as they were "finding themselves." During that period of life, they disavowed who they were and what they believed. Often, they have undergone much unnecessary pain and strain. In time, however, they arrive at a point where they yearn and value what they left behind. Unfortunately, in many cases, it may have cost them dearly to arrive at that wise assessment. Embracing and internalizing the core values of Adventism will equip them to face the stormy years that adolescence brings, and thus, sparing them from potentially shipwrecking their faith.

Vitality of Walls: For more than 100 years, Jerusalem's walls were merely rubble. If God was to have a city of refuge for His people, He needed to awaken them to the task of the day. That, He did. He raised and brought out of the Persian Empire a group of gritty individuals who purposed to do precisely that. Their historic role within Israel's history was such that the prophet Isaiah had laudable words written about them.

> Your people will build the ancient ruins
> and raise up the age-old foundations;
> you will be called Repairer of Broken Walls
> Restorer of Streets with Dwellings. (Isa. 58:12, NIV)

What an awesome privilege was theirs! They would repair that which Israel's enemies had torn down. That privilege is ours today as well, as we build up spiritual Jerusalem.

A Holy Haven: The church is to be a haven from the stress and strain of the world. It is also to be a place of safety. Its protective walls are to provide shelter and assurance. The accuser of the brethren should be held at bay as the body of Christ works harmoniously within. Such safety should simply be a by-product of the harmony found amongst the congregants that simply does not allow access for the devil to creep inside.

The church, also known as a sanctuary, is a refuge to those who are fleeing from Satan. Needless to say, there is prevailing danger as one ventures outside the compound. For it is primarily out there that Satan moves about at will. However, inside the gates, there needs to be a climate that is conducive to Christian growth and maturity. Indeed, we should be taking advantage of every possible opportunity to learn the ways of the enemy so that we can overcome his vicious attacks.

Community: Within the walls of the sanctuary, we need to experience community. Webster defines community as "a group of people with common characteristics or interest living together within the larger society." Community bonds people. It connects individuals in a manner that fosters brotherhood amongst them. That sense of community thrives in the spiritual realm because of the emphasis on sharing and caring for one another. The walls for a community are a sense of oneness—an identity that crisscrosses across generational, racial, and social lines and meshes them into a larger, unique body. It is the feeling of "one for all; and all for one" that is often expressed by professional team athletes.

Outside the Walls: However, that is not to say that we should never venture out of the city walls. In fact, we *need* to intentionally step outside to make contacts with those on the outside. There needs to be specific and intentional strategies to reach out to those who are struggling and straggling outside of our safe compound. Using another metaphor, the church is to be a beacon on a hill, lighting the path for others to find their way home. However, a light will not save—it only illuminates. Jesus is the Savior, and we must endeavor to make Him known to others.

Rubbish: As the wall-builders assembled to begin their assigned duties, they were immediately confronted with the rubbish that slowed down their progress (see Neh. 4:10). What was the rubbish? Obviously, years of neglect in many parts of the city had precipitated portions of the walls to weaken and fall. Dwellings that had been unoccupied for decades also caved in. Also, let us remind ourselves that the onslaught of the Babylonian army had left the city devastated. Needless to say, the debris had to be removed before moving forward with the reconstruction of the wall.

Today's Rubbish: Today, we seem to be surrounded by rubbish, and we need to keep it at a distance. It seems that our society feeds on rubbish. Most television programs, movies, and even most of the so-called "family entertainment" can be categorized as rubbish. Popular musical performers and comics alike, also hurl their lewd and suggestive expressions into the ears of a passive and receptive culture. Since our society has a voracious appetite for entertainment, it is daily feeding upon the vulgarity and sexual innuendos constantly being bombarded by the mass media. Such corruptive entertainment is extremely harmful for those who are citizens of Zion. It is nearly impossible to move forward spiritually while feeding upon that type of trash. Exposure to such entertainment will be at one's spiritual risk. And that's no laughing matter.

Chapter 9
Enemies

As we have already seen, whenever God initiates His work, opposition arises. As the project to build the house of God was moving forward, enemies were watching from a distance. It would simply be a matter of time when they would make their distaste for the project known. Initially, they did not consider the project feasible. In their analysis, there was little chance for success. It was their desire that the entire operation would undergo significant setbacks culminating in a full retreat.

Nevertheless, the spirit that drove the Jews across 900 miles of desert terrain back to their homeland would not allow them to withdraw that easily. They had come too far to simply whimper and walk away. No, theirs was a holy task. The temple needed to be built, and they would do it even in the face of *any* opposition.

Infiltration: One of the strategies that the enemy wanted to use was infiltration. A delegation was sent to the worksite and sought permission to work alongside the temple-builders. The consensus within the Jewish camp was a resounding no. The Samaritans, the group that had offered to help, reacted with bitterness. Not to be deterred, they would seek other avenues to stifle the progress.

Political Arm: Since their initial strategy did not bear any fruit, they decided to retaliate using their political connections. One of their first and more strident moves was to write a letter to the center of provincial operations in Susa. The message and tone of the communique aimed at casting the temple builders in a very negative light before the king. Accusations were made of a potential revolt by the Jews in their quest to establish an independent state. Simply stated, they maligned the entire project and cast the Jews as traitors to the monarchy (see Ezra 4).

Legalities: Additionally, they implied that the émigrés had no legal authority to rebuild the city. The accusers challenged the Persian officials to check the royal annals that would allegedly confirm their allegations. It was a serious allegation drawn against the people of God. However, the Jews were not disheartened. When the imperial chronicles were consulted, they revealed no red flags against them (see Ezra 6:1–2). Everything that was being done had been royally decreed. In fact, the inquiry revealed that the project had the financial backing of the imperial coffers.

Calm and Steady: The calm and mature fashion in which the temple and wall builders reacted under such an array of opposition and obstacles, conveyed a message to their neighbors. The message was that theirs was not simply another city being rebuilt—they were building a city for their God and His temple. Such conviction continued to alarm, confuse, and infuriate the enemy. Although every effort mustered against the sons of Israel had failed, yet the enemy would continue relentlessly to oppose the project.

Sarcasm: Another approach embraced by the enemies of Israel took the form of sarcasm. By that medium the project was painted as something that was beyond realistic expectations; merely wishful thinking that was not based on present realities. The desired goal of such quips and criticisms was to downgrade morale and foster a spirit of defeatism among the builders. Try as they did, the sarcasm and irony did not dampen the morale one iota. That, in turn, made the enemy furious. Feeling that they were losing the psychological battle as well, they now moved to more direct forms of confrontation.

Treachery and Violence: Treachery and violence were the new weapons. In an effort to put teeth to their sinister plan, Nehemiah was invited to leave the safety of the city and to meet with them at Ono. The meeting point was a village located twenty miles north of Jerusalem. One can detect that the plan had danger written all over it. Why would he leave the safety of the city and venture out to a distant town to meet with his enemies? On the other hand, if Nehemiah did not attend the meeting at Ono, that action could be misconstrued to imply that he was afraid to confront his accusers. Wisely, the governor declined the invitation.

Threats: But the enemies were persistent. The following strategy involved intimidation. A letter was sent to Nehemiah with a veiled threat. It stated that his life was in certain danger, and thus, he should seek shelter in the temple. His response is worth analyzing. He could have shown restraint; after all, his life *was* in danger. He did not do that. Had he done so, Nehemiah would have communicated to the entire outpost that there were serious reasons to be fearful. But he simply refused to show his fears and declined the suggestion that he hide in the temple. By refusing to play into their ploy, he minimized the panic and fearmongering within the community (see Neh. 6).

Extortion: In their ongoing quest of trying to rattle Nehemiah, they also used extortion. The threat was that they were going to go public with damaging information that they had secured on the project leader. The salient point of the accusation was that he was working behind the scenes to lead a revolt against Persia and proclaim himself king of the Jews (see Neh. 2:19; 6:6–7). It was a farfetched accusation. As with all of the tactics, its aim was to crush the spirit of the Jewish leader. Once again, Nehemiah wisely did not fall for it.

Let us take a closer look at the enemies of Israel in this pivotal era. The biblical record has left us the names of the four leading enemies who were creating all of this commotion against God's people.

Sanballat: As soon as the Jews embarked on the mission of rebuilding the walls of Jerusalem, Sanballat is found spearheading the opposition. As governor of Samaria, located on the northern flank of Jerusalem, he flouted a certain amount of power against the newly-arrived Jews. Why was he so scornful against the Jews and their mission? Perhaps, as a Samaritan, he viewed a rebuilt Jerusalem as a place that could draw worshippers away from their own holy site (see John 4:20). Whatever the reason may have been, Sanballat was forceful and vehement in his opposition to the reconstruction project. He wasted little time to manifest his disdain for the Jews and their project of reconstruction (see Neh. 4:1–2).

> *As soon as the Jews embarked on the mission of rebuilding the walls of Jerusalem, Sanballat is found spearheading the opposition.*

Tobiah: Alongside Sanballat, there was another official who usually seconded his opposition to the rebirth of Jerusalem. Tobiah was the governor of Ammon, the region east of Jerusalem, on the other side of the Jordan River. His immediate goal was to deter and frustrate the rebuilding of the walls. As historical enemies of Israel, the Ammonites were ready to do whatever was at their hands to make life difficult for the Jews. Centuries of war and strife had fostered hatred and disdain between the two peoples. His favorite weapon was to excoriate the entire project with sarcasm (see Neh. 4:3).

Geshem: Yet, there was another enemy, this one lying to the south of Jerusalem. The biblical record calls Geshem an Arab. He shared the very same aim of Sanballat and Tobiah—that the walls of Jerusalem should not be rebuilt (see Neh. 2:19). Frustrated that none of their stalling tactics were bearing fruit, they joined up to hatch up an assassination plot to take out Nehemiah (see Neh. 6:1–2).

Ashdod: The fourth enemy lay to the west of Israel, between the Mediterranean Sea and Israel proper. Ashdod was an old Philistine city that had survived many barrages and now joined the coalition against Jerusalem (see Neh. 4:7–8). Its roots were Philistine, and thus, it was perhaps driven by a deep-seated resentment that Israel had overtaken and settled their ancestral lands.[16]

Sellouts: Surprisingly, the enemies of God's people managed to maintain themselves fully informed as to events that were taking place within Jerusalem. How did they achieve that? It was accomplished by bribing people on the inside who acted as informants. These were individuals who had cast their integrity aside and had become sellouts. Shamelessly, they would let out the secrets of God's cause to the enemy. That resulted in the enemy having sufficient inside information so as to physically harm the population of the compound. That, in turn, produced angst and discouragement among those engaged in the building project.

Spiritual Application

As Christians, we are at odds with the ways of the world. We are definitely in contention with their worldview, entertainment, and values. Hence, we are not to be surprised that there will be tension as we try to build the church of Christ within the shadows of such a secular society.

Persecution: Persecution is the response of individuals toward another component of society when they are unable to control or diminish their activity or influence. It has been used throughout history by the dominant culture to dominate others. The apostle Paul warned the church that it would invariably face persecution (see 2 Tim. 3:12). Christianity has experienced such waves of persecution during various phases of its history. Yet, some have concluded that given the enlightened and tolerant worldviews that are prevalent today, such carnages as we read in the history books are highly unlikely today. In light of biblical prophetic insights, such a conclusion is erroneous. The book of Revelation warns in no uncertain terms that as the history of this planet reaches its climax, a certain group of people will be persecuted. Their crime will simply be that they hold a moral and religious stance that is countercultural (see Rev. 13).

---

[16]*The Seventh-day Adventist Bible Commentary* (Washington D.C.: Review and Herald Publishing Association, 1956), Vol. 3, 409.

At that period of history, some believers will consider the cost and conclude that it bears a dire price tag. Better to curtail the behavior and the expressions so as to not offend the dominant culture. Others, however, will not be deterred and will proceed to proclaim God's last message of mercy. Those taking the position of integrity, loyalty, and faith will be further harassed and ostracized. Yes, at that time, it will be extremely clear that those who do not join the rest of society in their form of worship will be persecuted. They will be labeled enemies of the state and will be prosecuted before magistrates. The opposition will use legal and strong-arm tactics to intimidate and manipulate believers. Yes, history does tend to travel the same path it has traveled in the past. It will be historical *déjà vu*.

Allurements: Nehemiah's enemies wanted to lure him away from the safety of Jerusalem. It was a bold-faced trap when they invited him to Ono. The enemy has used such strategy throughout history and is likewise using it today. The strategy is to lure the believer away from his faith base. Once that occurs, the individual is aimless and without a sense of community, and thus, easily manipulated. Warning: it is dangerous to abandon the security and blessings that the church family offers. When we venture out, we are placing ourselves on dangerous terrain. We need to realize the beauty and strength of our spiritual base and maintain a healthy distance from the enemy.

Distractions: Nehemiah's opposers also used distractions. Those were meant to create havoc, promote ill-feelings, and foment distrust. They were subtle in nature and yet had the potential of creating a major rift among the already-distressed builders. Rumors fit under the heading of distractions. They are usually hearsay going from one person to another and lacking full validation as far as sourcing. Yet, they can distract and thus divert the passion and energy of the person that is being criticized.[17]

---

[17]Rumors have certain unique characteristics. Charles R. Swindoll reminds us what some of those traits are: The sources are never given; rumors are pregnant with exaggeration and inaccuracy, and gullible listeners will feed upon them and pass them on. See Charles R. Swindoll, *Hand Me Another Brick: How Effective Leaders Motivate Themselves and Others* (Nashville, TN.: Thomas Nelson, Inc., 1998), 116–117.

Similarly, the world is constantly trying to distract the Christian believer and equally dissuade him from the mission. Such distractions are subtle set-ups meant to steer him away from engaging in our *raison d'ĕtre*—the reason for our existence—which is to build up the church of Christ while proclaiming His second coming. As someone has aptly phrased it: the main thing is to keep the main thing the main thing. The devil is keenly aware of how much damage that could unleash on his kingdom, and thus, works diligently to divert our attention from the main thing.

You may recall sitting on some church board where seemingly endless amount of time was spent on trivial matters that had no bearing on the core mission of the church. How sad, when it should be totally the opposite; the bulk of the time of any church board should be invested in planning and strategizing some form of outreach.[18] We must keep our eyes on the main thing—building up God's kingdom.

Reaction Within: When Nehemiah's enemies recognized that one strategy proved ineffective, they quickly moved on to another. That is much the same way the enemy functions today. When one form of attack does not work, he simply changes tactics. When verbal jabs do not obtain the desired results, the enemy turns to another distraction. These can be worship styles, music genres, administrative technicalities, and theological debates. Endless amount of time, energy, and resources are spent, while the main thing is sadly neglected.

Swords: Eventually, the enemy will turn to outright force as a means of quelling the people of God. During Nehemiah's time, measures were taken to have the people ready to ward off enemy attacks. Able-bodied men were given swords. All were expected to be vigilant. As they worked on the walls, the swords became

---

[18]"Work of the Board—Planning evangelism in all its phases. Since evangelism is the primary work of the church, the first item on the agenda of each church board meeting is to relate directly to the evangelization of the outreach (missionary) territory of the church. In addition, once each quarter of the year the entire church board meeting can well be devoted to plans for evangelism. The board will study local field committee recommendations for evangelistic programs and methods. It will determine how these can best be implemented by the church. The pastor and the church board will initiate and develop plans for public evangelistic campaigns." *Seventh-day Adventist Church Manual* (Hagerstown, MD.: Review and Herald Publishing Association, 2000), 83.

reliable companions. The work progressed, but in large part, it was due to the fact that within the walls of Jerusalem, the people had armed themselves (see Neh. 4).

Surely, we hope for a future without stress or strain. However, that is merely wishful thinking since those who oppose God will eventually attack His followers. The double-edged sword will then become for us a trusted source of strength (see Heb. 4:12). The promises found in the Bible need to be internalized and become part of our thinking and self-defense. It was so with our Lord, and we should also model His winning strategy.

However, let me add that a superficial knowledge of some key texts is not what we are talking about. It needs to be a real encounter experience with the God of the Bible. The Bible is a testimony about our Lord. It is simply a record of how He has been faithful to His promises throughout history. It is where we come face to face with Him who is our refuge and strength in times of trouble (see Ps. 46:1). Plainly said, there is no substitute for wholesome Bible study. When I was a young man growing up in church, I was challenged to study the Bible, and I did. I memorized names of rivers and mountains and obscure personalities to show that I really *knew* the Bible. In time, I realized that such information lacked relevancy and transformational impact. Thankfully, I have moved beyond that and read its pages to have an encounter with the Savior.

Trumpet: In his autobiographical record, Nehemiah records that during the crisis, he had a trumpeter with him at all times (see Neh. 4:18). Should an imminent danger be detected, his task was to sound the alarm and alert the compound. Subconsciously, every laborer was attuned to the potential sound of the trumpet. Even when engaged in the construction, their ears were attentive to the airwaves so as to decipher any trumpet sound. With prior instructions, everyone knew exactly their function at the sound of the trumpet. Thus, the entire body was forewarned and was ready to react.[19]

---

[19]Trumpets were commonly used throughout Israel's history, and thus, their ears were trained to pick up its sounds. In fact, one of their yearly feasts was the Feast of Trumpets. See Numbers 10:1–10 and Leviticus 23:24–25.

As toilers in the Lord's vineyard, we need to be fully attuned to the sound of the trumpet. Soon it will sound. And it will indicate to us that the labor has been completed. Spiritual Jerusalem has been built; the work has been found finished. Then our ears will be alerted by the sound of the final trumpet. It will convey that the time has arrived—the time to pack and go. Having been told that "no one knows the day or hour," we need to double-up and rebuild the city. There is no time to waste. Let us work while fully attuned to the final trumpet (see 1 Thess. 4:16).

Chapter 10

Unequally Yoked (Defining Who You Are...)

Ezra: In 457 BC, Ezra arrived from Susa. His arrival was welcomed like water in the desert. Apathy had set in amongst the settlers. Though the temple had been built, it was in the distant past, for it was fifty-eight years prior. Present reality was apathy. Morale was low. The big picture for the city of Jerusalem seemed murky. Accompanying Ezra were 8,000 additional dwellers, who arrived at a time when their presence would provide a much-needed morale booster for the locals.

Ezra, a devout student and expositor of the law, relished his role as a moral teacher for the inhabitants of Jerusalem and its hinterland. He wanted Israel to catch a glimpse of the glory of God. He figured that once that occurred, the people would forge forward into any daunting task. The settlers were quick to pick up the fact that Ezra was a moralist. Those who were like-minded among the settlers shared with him something that weighed heavily upon their hearts. In their eyes, God was withholding His blessings due to sin in the camp.

Mixed Marriages: The thorny issue that was causing a rift among the settlers was that of mixed marriages. Indeed, many a Jew had married non-Jewish women, and that was bringing discord among the settlers (Ezra 9:1). The fallout was that it was leading to an acceptance of lax moral living. Moreover, the ill was pervasive. Even people in leadership had fallen to the trend (Ezra 9:2). Those harping the position that the divisive situation was contrary to God's role for Israel stood on solid ground.

Centuries earlier, Yahweh had provided a dire warning of the consequences when marrying non-believers (see Exod. 34:11–16; Deut. 7:3–4). Logic was at the core of the admonition: a pagan spouse could potentially be an instrument in leading astray the believing partner. In addition, it was a failure to live up to the obligations of the covenant with Yahweh. Seen in that light, it was much more than simply marrying an outsider; it was open rebellion against the covenant with Yahweh. In spite of such clear warnings, many of the émigrés were following in that indefensible path. Apparently, the prevailing leadership had looked the other way and had not dealt with the issue at hand.

However, Ezra was not that type of leader. When the shocking news was broken to him, he was shaken to the core. He was in spiritual shock. The teacher/priest prostrated to the ground and wept. The shock was such that he remained in that position for hours. He was in full disbelief of what the people of Israel were doing in spite of their high calling (see Ezra 9:3–4).

He had come to rebuild the city and yet quickly realized that the moral component was at the core of the deplorable conditions. Appropriately, he shifted his emphasis. Addressing the moral lapse would have to take priority over building physical structures. For addressing the slippage of the settlers, God had procured an individual of great spiritual perception and integrity.

Soon thereafter, a committee was set up to examine the individual cases of the offenders. Those who had married non-believers came before the committee, and each case was decided on its own merits. Eventually, more than 100 mixed marriages were annulled. Needless to say, it was a horrible ordeal for the families involved. There were wailing and deep-seated agony of the soul. Nevertheless, it needed to be done, and Ezra led the process.[20]

Spiritual Application

Post-Christian: We live within a society that does not relish being told what to do. We thrive in our freedom and independence. American and Western cultures are post-Christian societies in their thinking. The word that scholars use is post-Christian. By ascribing such a haughty description, it is a proclamation that we are beyond the dogmas and traditions of Christianity. Its broader implication is that humanity has freed itself from God and His restrictive mores.

> *We live within a society that does not relish being told what to do. We thrive in our freedom and independence.*

Not surprisingly, society's present mindset is one that is on a warpath with traditional Christian values. The church, which exists within the confinements of modern society, is affected by the constant bombardment from the secular-minded front. Therefore, even within the body of Christ, many do not want to hear about marrying only believers. No; they are impatient and slight any teaching that seemingly curtails their freedom. Lest we forget, God always has our best interest in mind. Consequently, His admonitions are based on that principle. The counsel of the Lord continues to be that Christians should not marry non-believers because it will adversely affect their spirituality and potentially their salvation (Amos 3:3).

A House Divided: A house divided cannot stand; and that is transparently evident in the case of marriage. That can easily be seen when one parent holds to one set of spiritual values and the other does not. Such incongruity is a set-up for polarization. Given the already mounting challenges of rearing children in a

---
[20]J. G. McConville, *Ezra, Nehemiah, and Esther* (Philadelphia: The Westminster Press, 1985), 68–71.

post-Christian society, we should not add any additional baggage to the equation. It would be catastrophic to have moral discrepancies within the same household. That is the perfect recipe of confusion for the children. Many homes today are battlefields of right vs wrong and moral vs immoral. In part that is so because of the life-partner that was chosen. Secular viewpoints will consistently clash with Christian principles of child-rearing; since each represents diametrical philosophies of life. For a number of decades, I have been around young couples. I have counseled them; married them; studied the Bible with them and held couples' meetings for them. Consequently, I have heard way too many cries of the soul by partners decrying the anguish and divide they experience while living with espouses who were unbelievers. The day-to-day grind in such a marriage, can become unbearable. The sum total of such relationships that did not follow biblical guidelines, is that of marriages that are barely standing.

Needless to say, the counsel of the Lord is still very much applicable today: do not marry outside of the faith. The children will unintentionally bear some of the adverse by-products of such a marriage (Ezra 10). Hindsight is very useful; yet it always late. The case studies that have been reproduced in the Bible—Esau, Samson, Solomon—are meant for us to glean valuable lessons and not relive their pitfalls. Let us follow the counsel of the Word of God in this matter and we will be on the path of having healthier marriages (2 Chronicles 20:20).

Chapter 11
Populating the City

We have already seen that the Spirit-led ministry of Nehemiah, coupled with that of Ezra, bore rapid and amazing results (see chapter 8, Building the Walls). Within fifty-two days, the walls had been reconstructed. It was undeniable that the year 444 BC was a banner year for the gritty settlers of Jerusalem. Now they could look forward to the next phase—making Zion the lively and bustling city that it had once been.

People Needed: Having conquered a major obstacle, the leadership realized that they had an unforeseen issue that needed their immediate attention. The hinterland, with its open space for houses and crops, had become the dwelling region for many of the returnees. Consequently, the city was sparsely settled. It was visibly obvious to the leadership that the now-refurbished city urgently needed warm bodies to transform itself into a viable and vibrant municipality.

Thus, leadership was forced to hammer out a plan to induce those in the outlying areas to come and populate Zion. It was readily obvious that a healthy number of residents had intentionally chosen to inhabit the outskirts of the city. Geographically, they were close to the metropolis, yet they were not part of it. The challenge for the leading minds was to entice them to dwell within the recently-renovated town. Such people were the very first ones targeted as potential citizens for the city that now offered security within its walls.

Plenty of People: The precise number of potential inhabitants in the surrounding areas is not known. Guesses range from 50,000 to 100,000. In either case, the potential was tremendous. At this point one may wonder why they had chosen to live outside of the hub. For one thing, up until that point, the city had been vulnerable—it had no walls. A city without walls was simply an open target, even for the weakest enemies. Additionally, the city had been devastated by the Babylonian army, and for a number of decades, it was merely a heap of rubble. There was debris, fallen structures, and multiple eyesores in every direction. That was the mental picture that many had of Jerusalem, an unattractive and even dangerous place to live.

Heavy Demands: Another factor that may have kept dwellers at a distance was their sense of independence. A city in the condition of Jerusalem demanded an overly amount of vigilance and sacrifice from its citizens. That could only be remedied by able-bodied individuals willing to devote a good portion of their time and energy to that end. Living in Jerusalem was a form of sacrificial living. In that light, many may have sensed that their independence and lifestyle would be curtailed by simply living in the city. Additionally, Jerusalem yet lacked the infrastructure to house a large population group. Thus, we can understand the hesitation on the part of some to make Jerusalem their permanent home.[21]

Outside Dangers: In spite of the challenges of city dwelling, country living was no picnic either. One of the dynamics of the era was that the countryside was frequently attacked by marauders. When such onslaughts were perceived to be in the works, the

---
[21]Swindoll, *Hand Me Another Brick*, 161–163.

population of the hinterland would seek shelter in the nearby walled cities. For an oncoming military force, only a walled city provided a viable defense. Since Jerusalem lacked such defenses, there was no appeal to move there. However, once the walls were up, that was no longer an excuse. What one perceives is that they wanted to maintain their independent living and yet have access to the shelter of the city whenever distress would visit.

Response: As mentioned above, there was ample space within the city, and yet it remained strikingly empty (see Neh. 7:4–5). Yet, those living outside of the city were at risk from the enemies that roamed the area. That led to the Jerusalem council asking for people to voluntarily abandon their country homes and venture to live within the city. As readers removed in time and culture, one does not fully grasp the tension of what it must have meant for those families to uproot themselves and relocate inside the city. Being self-sustaining farmers or shepherds, their livelihood largely depended on their proximity to the land. By moving into the city, their *modus vivendi* had to be re-oriented. In some cases, the land had been held by the family for generations, and there were, understandably, emotional ties to the land.

The biblical record indicates that a fair number of families decided to relocate within the gates. At a time when the leadership of the city needed families to bolster the population and to provide a sense of security to the entire citizenry, these families stepped forward and did exactly that. Their noble action was highly appreciated, and the written record attests to that (see Neh. 11:1–2).

Join Us: In addition to those who voluntarily had come to dwell in Jerusalem, the leadership felt that there were others who could be asked directly to become dwellers of Zion. To achieve their goal, a form of draft was established. One of every ten inhabitants living around the circumference of the capital city was asked to relocate within the city. Again, the response was positive, and the project was achieved successfully (see Neh. 11).

With the temple in full operation, the walls up, and a sizeable population safely within its gates, Jerusalem was back in business. It was a good moment for the city that had experienced so much havoc in recent history. Happy days were back again!

Spiritual Application

The Church: The church has been compared to a city—the city of God (see Heb. 12:22–23). A city is not an easy enterprise to operate. It takes a significant number of talented people to fill all of the pivotal positions that are needed to operate it day and night. As a city grows numerically, it is also enriched culturally. New inhabitants bring their creative capacities and cultural uniqueness and thus, enrich the overall composition of a metropolis.

As God's church, we also have a mandate to increase the population within the city of the Lord. One of the parables that Jesus shared with His disciples dealt with an invitation to a great banquet. Yet, the guests excuse themselves and do not honor the invitation. The man who had prepared the banquet is understandably upset, and thus, orders his servants:

> Go out quickly into the streets and alleys of the town and bring in the poor, the crippled, the blind and the lame. "Sir," the servant said, "what you ordered has been done, but there is still room." Then the master told his servant, "Go out to the roads and country lanes and make them come in, so that my house will be full." (Luke 14:21–23, NIV).

New Blood: Newcomers to a congregation bring much-needed vitality. Their recent conversion experience is in itself an enriching component to the church family. Additionally, the pool of backgrounds and life experiences adds variety to the entire mosaic. Furthermore, due to their unique perspectives regarding their conversion experience and personal narrative, newcomers bring their own individual skill sets that, needless to say, enrich the overall congregation.

Experts in church growth speak of a point in the history of congregations in which the numerical growth reaches a plateau. Obviously, the following phase is a numerical decrease. In time, they may find themselves very busy "doing church" but hardly ever seeing anyone joining it.[22] A congregation like that would benefit immensely from new blood.

---
[22]Gladden, *Plant the Future*, 28–32.

Spirit-Led Journeys: I have had the wonderful privilege of leading hundreds of souls by way of Bible study and evangelism to embrace Jesus as their Savior. Additionally, I have instilled in them the biblical worldview and the Adventist lifestyle. Some of those individuals have nearly begged to be baptized into the faith. They had been on a spiritual quest, and when exposed to the beauty and logic of Adventism, they felt they were finally home. Here is one such story.

Michelle (not her real name) learned about the Sabbath through a non-Adventist publication. She decided to keep it, and for months, she kept it by herself in her apartment. A friend of Michelle's invited her to our church, and she rejoiced to find an entire congregation that kept the biblical Sabbath. It was a pleasure to study the Bible with her. She was ready and willing to embrace anything and everything that the Lord Jesus would ask. In time, she and her husband were baptized and became fully engaged and an inspiration to our church body.

Different Journeys: Others, however, require long and exhaustive hours of Bible study.

People do not always perceive what they are missing in their spiritual lives, and thus, one has to help them arrive at the phase of self-discovery. Bible studies follow, and gradually, they embrace the message and join the gospel family. Though arriving by way of different paths, both of these groups end up in the same body as fellow believers. Again, it is also a joy to work with those souls and witness their growth as they discover and embrace new doctrinal gems.

One such individual was Milton (again, not his real name). His wife was visiting the church. Upon learning about it, he asked her to stop attending. She stopped for a while and then suggested, "Why don't you come with me and assess this whole church thing?" He acceded. They came, and wisely, she led him to the front row— he had to be attentive through the evangelistic meetings. In time, he opened up, and we began Bible studies. Though it was a slow and methodical process, he embraced the Lord and was baptized along with his wife and son. Such individuals, though tough to get through to them, once they come through, they embrace the message with heart and soul.

The Field: God wants His church to be active in the realm of soulwinning. There are millions living within shouting distance of our church walls. Other millions have a running acquaintance with the church. It is imperative that we capitalize on such relationships and proximities for the kingdom of God. I am shaken to the core when I read what Leonard Ravenhill has written:

> The masses are at the very doors of our churches—not won because they haven't been reached; not reached because they are not loved. Thank God for all that is being done by the foreign missions. Yet, it is very strange that we can become "apparently" very concerned for the people on the other side of the world, and not for our neighbors who perish just across the street.[23]

Pained People: There are others who have abandoned the safety of our walls. They used to worship with us but have left our fellowship. There are millions of former Adventists throughout the world. Some have latent issues of resentment and will find it very difficult to come back. But it behooves us to try to bring them back within the fold. At one point they had a heart for the message, and we know that the Holy Spirit can certainly reignite the flame and assuage any lingering aches.

> *The masses are at the very doors of our churches—not won because they haven't been reached; not reached because they are not loved.*

I will share one such story. Randon (not his real name) was a young Adventist. In his youth, he drifted away, and the church disfellowshipped him. He felt that no serious effort was ever made to reclaim him. In his eyes the entire process lacked genuine Christian love. Thus, he left the fellowship entirely. For the next twenty years, he was totally out there. He met a young lady, and they began living together while starting a family. In the course of time, Melissa (again, not her real name) became

---
[23]Quoted in Randy Maxwell's, *Bring Back the Glory: What Happens When God's People Pray for Revival*, (Nampa, ID.: Pacific Press Publishing Association, 2000), 102.

acquainted with Adventism. Ironically, she grew to the point that she wanted to join the church. When we met, he shared his deep-seated anger and disdain for the people who had done him wrong. We talked for a long time. I apologized for the lack of human empathy displayed twenty years back. However, my aim was to make him see that after twenty years, the other side had moved on and that he also needed to do the same. The Holy Spirit came to my aid, and he softened. Then came the breakthrough. Soon, the bitter ex-member joined his wife in marriage and their sons into the watery grave. The past was forgotten, and truly a new life had begun for them.

Invite Them: However, in order for the church to capitalize on all of the aforementioned interest components, it needs to become more intentional in its approach. The categories mentioned above are people who already have, to varying degrees, some type of rapport with the church. If we were to reach out to them, using multiple avenues, and make our churches more embracing and receptive to such individuals, we could potentially expect millions of people coming into our churches. Remember, they are just outside of our walls.

I am utterly thrilled every time I read the description of the mission of the church that follows:

> The church is God's appointed agency for the salvation of men. It was organized for service, and its mission is to carry the gospel to the world ... The church is the repository of the riches of the grace of Christ; and through the church will eventually be made manifest ... the final and full display of the love of God ... The church is God's fortress, His city of refuge, which He holds in a revolted world ... It is the theater of His grace, in which He delights to reveal His power to transform hearts.[24]

It is primarily on the inside, within the walls of spiritual Jerusalem, that such miracles are taking place. I have seen my fair share of them and rejoice every time I am made aware of how the

---

[24]Ellen G. White, *The Acts of the Apostles,* (Mountain View, CA.: Pacific Press Publishing Association, 1911), 9–12.

gospel proclamation is transforming lives. Let us strive to make our churches such soulwinning enterprises. May our churches become such hotbeds of transformation that the enemy will have to warn his followers: Stay away from that church; you enter at your own risk!

Chapter 12

Prophetic Guidance

The Jewish exile into Babylon was a shattering experience for Yahweh's people. Not only were they driven from their God-chosen land, but their capital city was utterly destroyed. Their two leading institutions—priesthood and monarchy—were truncated. Such devastating events led many to question God's guidance upon the nation. On the other hand, the staggering devastation of Jerusalem—a fulfillment of prophetic utterance—led others to unquestionably embrace more than ever the prophetic directives.

Prophetic Fulfillment: There was great expectation among the exiles as they perceived that the seventy years of captivity, announced by Jeremiah, were coming to their end. The anticipation was that God would once again make a big splash in bringing His people back to their homeland. However, as it turned out, God would work by way of the pagan Persian kings. Accordingly, it was Cyrus who, in the year 537 BC, issued a royal decree allowing all Jews to return to their ancestral homeland in Palestine. Additionally, they would be allowed to rebuild the city and its temple. Even the temple utensils in Persian custody would be returned. To top it off, the royal treasury would cover the bulk of the reconstruction expenses. (see Ezra 6:1–5; Isa. 44:28).

Departure: The prophet Daniel, who had practically spent all of his life in exile, was likely present to see his countrymen embark on a historic enterprise—to build a city. He may have recalled how he had taken hold of Jeremiah's prophecy to instill hope in the hearts of his fellow Jews (see Dan. 9:1–19). Now he was witnessing the fulfillment of prophecy, and his brethren were literally going home. As the prophet who had foretold the fall of Jerusalem, Jeremiah was now being given his just due for having properly prophesied the return from exile as well (see Jer. 25:11–14).

Arrival: The huge caravan trudged the 900 miles of desert terrain that eventually took them to their destination. In the summer of 536 BC, they arrived at Jerusalem. They were greeted by a ghostly, devastated city. That was not a surprise. They knew that Jerusalem lay in ruins. The immediate months were spent setting up shop—land was cleared, and houses were built. There was urgency due to the oncoming winter season—with its rain and cold weather. Come springtime, they would start rebuilding the city and its temple in earnest.

Small Beginnings: Indeed, as spring rolled around, the sound of tools filled the air. Grand expectations abounded. As the temple's cornerstone is being placed, the Levites and priests joyfully lead the congregation in praises. Yet, for a minority amongst them, it was not a time of joy—it was a time of anguish. Who were they? It was a small group of residents who had lived through the exile and thus had literally seen Solomon's glorious temple before its demise. Now, they are overtaken by angst, anger, and guilt as they envision the strident difference between the glorious edifice of their memory and what seems to be a puny building that is to take its place. (see Hag. 2:3).

The incident, which took place in the spring of 535 BC, had an immediate and negative impact on the would-be temple builders. The upbeat spirit that had characterized the enterprise thus far whittled away fast. Construction on the temple premises came to a halt. Many rationalized that it was not yet in God's time to rebuild (see Hag. 1:2). Consequently, for the next fifteen years, the work that had begun with much fanfare was ignored. In time, weeds began to grow on the temple compound, and the project was non-existent.

Whenever God's people are advancing God's agenda, the enemy steps in and will make every effort to halt its progress. In our narrative, he accomplished that by the stalemate that resulted at groundbreaking. The wailing and lackluster attitude displayed there deflated the momentum of the men who were working against all odds to erect the temple. That was followed by discouragement. People who were already risking their lives did not need that type of behavior from amongst their own. The lack of sensitivity by those who minimized the second temple eventually led to the entire project collapsing.

Malaise: With no temple project, there was a shift in the energy and passion of the settlers. The order of the day was making a living and surviving in the parched Palestinian terrain. Momentum had shifted. The passion that had brought them from Persia was now sadly lost. Saddest of all was to realize that the malaise was not brought on by outside forces, but by the "brethren" from within. The years spent in making a living and surviving added up to fifteen. Zerubbabel, the political leader, is understandably frustrated by the prevalent apathy. Fifteen years of his life had come to naught. Joshua, the spiritual leader, was also in the dumps. Malaise had infected everyone, even leadership.

Prophets: Yet, the true temple builder was God. Now, He moved to remedy the tenuous situation. This He did by raising up a couple of prophets—Haggai and Zechariah—who would bring timely messages to stir the disengaged settlers into action. You may recall that in chapter 7 (Completion of the Temple), we discussed the crucial and vital roles they played in inspiring the beleaguered Israelites to move forward.

The prophetic utterances paid off. The people's spirit was buoyed to do God's bidding. Once they began, they worked with fervor and efficiency. Emotion and newly-minted excitement were once again in their midst. Indeed, the Holy Spirit was powerfully echoing the words of the prophets, and the people responded with willing hearts. The marshaled émigrés were so moved that within five years—March 12, 515 BC—the structure had been completed.

Spiritual Application

Parallel Mission: Similarly, today, we also have a compelling mission. It is to build up God's church through the proclamation of the gospel. Let us recall that in the process of building up the temple, God's people faced many obstacles: low morale, outside enemies, internal strife, and government intervention. It is likewise today. As Zerubbabel, we have been at the task long enough and have not yet completed the mission. The challenge is compounded with every passing year. Clearly, a mighty closing push is sorely needed. Aware of our predicament, God has raised a prophetic voice within our midst.

The Adventist Movement: The prophetic last-day remnant church of Revelation 12 had specific characteristics that set it aside from other religious bodies. Firstly, it would emerge after 1798, following the conclusion of the prophetic 1260-year period. Secondly, it would keep the commandments of God and give the Sabbath its proper place within its message. Thirdly, it would be blessed with the prophetic gift. In the early 1840s, the Adventist movement made huge inroads into the popular psyche of America. Throngs, primarily in the northeast region of the country, were impacted by the message of a soon-coming Lord. The movement made such an impact on the general population that it has garnered a designation—that of being part of the Second Great Awakening in American history. Then came 1844—the year of the disappointment. The movement was devastated at the realization that Jesus had not come. There was mass confusion, criticism, and collapse. It was a deplorable time to believe the Adventist message.

Ellen G. White: In December of 1844, a seventeen-year-old young lady of Portland, Maine, had a vision in which she saw the Adventist believers steadily marching toward the celestial city. It was a vision from God to uplift and buoy His depressed people.

Initially, her gift was questioned, but eventually, it was examined and confirmed, for it met the biblical criteria. Thus, Ellen G. Harmon (White after her marriage in 1846) began an illustrious prophetic ministry for the Seventh-day Adventist Church that lasted till her death in 1915. Throughout her seventy-year ministry, she offered the church and private individuals prudent counsel in many areas of life. All in all, she was able to inspire and guide a disheartened band of believers into a worldwide community of believers that today encircles the globe. Much of what the church accomplished in its formative years was spearheaded directly or indirectly by Ellen G. White and her prophetic ministry. Once again, history repeated itself as a discouraged band of believers were aroused to action by a prophetic voice.[25]

---

[25]There is a host of material on the rise of Adventism and the role of Ellen G. White within its formation. Thus, I have selected two such works; one almost exclusively by non-Adventists scholars and the other by an Adventist historian. Edwin Scott Gaustad, ed., *The Rise of Adventism: A Commentary on the Social and Religious Ferment of Mid-Nineteenth Century America* (San Francisco: Harper and Row, Publishers, 1974); George R. Knight, *Millennial Fever and the End of the World: A Comprehensive Survey of Millerism and America's Fascination with the Millennium in the Nineteenth Century* (Boise, ID.: Pacific Press Publishing Association, 1993).

Chapter 13
Revival and Reformation

Nehemiah was endowed with endless energy and remarkable leadership skills that enabled him to rally a disheartened group of people into action. The end result exceeded all expectations. As has already been pointed out earlier, he was successful in completing the walls within fifty-two days. What an astonishing accomplishment! For decades the task had evaded an entire generation, and by the bold and decisive leadership of one individual, the project was completed in record time.

Walls Define: The erected wall provided more than physical protection. The enclosure of the city put some distance between Jerusalem and its pagan neighbors. In a subtle way, the walls guarded self-identity to a people surrounded by menacing enemies. You see, during the many years in which Israel had been eking out a living in Palestine, moral and spiritual compromises had taken place. Now, the walls served to minimize the interaction between Israel and its pagan neighbors, thus minimizing the exchange of corrosive influence.

A Solemn Convocation: At the completion of the project, Nehemiah and Ezra were fully aware that a wave of goodwill prevailed amongst the settlers. Jointly, they concluded that it was crucial to capitalize on the camaraderie that the completion of the wall project had infused within the camp.

What would be their strategy?

What began to shape in the minds of the forward-thinking leaders was to call for a special convocation. In that assembly the unique history of Israel and Yahweh's prominent role was to be recounted and extolled. Ezra, the aged and highly-respected scribe, would lead out in the reading and explanation of the Torah. As a godly rabbi viewed graciously by the congregants, he was the ideal expositor for the occasion.

Revival: Moreover, the occasion was solemn. A makeshift platform was erected. The congregation stood around it. With scroll in hand, the wise shepherd read the Inspired Word. There was rapt attention. Young and old made an earnest effort to capture the message of the Holy Writ. For those lacking adequate skills in the Hebrew language, translators were placed within the crowd to fully convey meaning to the words that were read and spoken. The reading lasted from morning till noon, yet the people remained engaged. By the afternoon, a sense of shame and betrayal began to take hold amongst the congregants. The Holy Spirit was finding access to their hearts. Outbursts of weeping were heard throughout the assembly. Sporadic heartfelt confessions poured forth from stricken souls. The people were indeed moved by the Word. Many saw their shortcomings through the angle of a much-needed new beginning. It was obvious that something unusual was taking place. What was it? A revival had broken out (see Neh. 8:9–12).

Reformation: The next day, there were again visible and audible manifestations by the Spirit of God. The conviction that the Spirit had wrought in the hearts of the congregants could not be quenched. Right then and there, they determined that they wanted to fully align their lives with God's statutes. Conviction gripped the hearts, and confessions were voiced. Men and women sought ways in which they could amend their lives so as to be in harmony with God's revelation. An immediate fruit of the revival was that the Feast of Tabernacles, which had long been neglected, now it was joyfully anticipated and celebrated. The revival also led to definitive action. A scroll was brought, and the people fixed their names to it. It was a covenant renewing their dedication toward Yahweh (see Neh. 8:13–18; 9:38).

The Spirit reminded them of three areas of gross national neglect. The areas were:

- Marriages: the counsel of not marrying pagans had not been faithfully followed
- Sabbath: the people had become careless and lax in their Sabbath observance
- Finances: financial commitment to the temple and its ministry was lacking

Nehemiah was the very first one to sign the document. Priests, Levites, and others in leadership roles joined in the rededication. Moreover, gatekeepers, singers, and temple attendants also came forth and seconded the actions of their leaders. It was clear; the revival had birthed a reformation. The reformation which ensued brought forth fruits of righteous and sacrificial living (see Neh. 10:28–39).

Spiritual Application

It is noteworthy that the concerns underscored at Jerusalem in 444 BC have plagued God's people throughout history. Today, they rank among the favorites in the enemy's arsenal. He fully understands that in order to debilitate God's fortress, he needs to aggressively assail those three areas. As one reads the account, one glaring lesson leaps from the narrative: the enemy despises wholesome marriages, he also attacks the Sabbath for it is a unique tie that binds believers around the planet, and, of course, he does not want money going to advance the kingdom

> *It is noteworthy that the concerns underscored at Jerusalem in 444 BC have plagued God's people throughout history.*

of God. History teaches lessons that we cannot overlook or minimize. Here are some obvious lessons for all of us.

Marriage: The devil's success rate in destroying marriages today is alarming. Marriages between believers and non-believers have some negative built-in trapping by its mere composition. When such marriages occur, the participants place themselves in potentially at-risk matrimonies. When the blueprint is not followed, it should not alarm us that such marriages may end up in divorce court. Moreover, marriages among God's people are also crumbling at a disturbing rate with little hesitation or post-mortem guilt by the parties involved. Additionally, little or no remorse is demonstrated by married couples when announcing their breakup. Then, it's simply on to their next romance.

I have known couples who exemplified the very best of marital etiquette, and unexpectedly they announce their separation and divorce. Nearly always, it is without biblical grounds. Any attempt at reconciliation by friends and family is brushed aside. Fearful of condemnation, they want to be left alone. When someone seeks to admonish them in love, the counsel is shunned. They simply do not want to hear a different tune than the one they are humming. Seemingly, without much remorse, they cast their marriage vows aside and see their marriage come to an end. Oh, how we need to heed the posture taken by the Jerusalem revival and registered for the church of the ages.

Sabbath Observance: Sabbath observance has been compromised and toned down as dominant social mores have intruded into the church. On the other hand, voices within the denomination, not wanting to be labeled archaic, legalistic, and out of touch, have urged easing off on the biblical standard for Sabbath observance. A succinct shift has taken place that views the Sabbath more as a rest day than as a holy day. Yet, the Lord of the Sabbath has not changed it; it is still His holy day. Living in the twenty-first century, with ever-busier schedules and gadgets to keep us occupied, we desperately need the peace and sanctity that the Sabbath day ushers.[26]

---

[26]"How fascinating, then, that thousands of years ago the Lord gave humanity a commandment designed to protect us from time's tyranny. God carved out an inviolable and

On a missionary trip to Cochabamba, Bolivia, I visited a church service being conducted in the Quechua tongue. Though I could not understand the language, I sensed and witnessed the joy that permeated the service. There was one phrase that I heard repeatedly throughout the service—*cusi sábado*. Inquiring as to the meaning of the phrase, Melinda (not her real name) told me that it meant Happy Sabbath. Her facial expression conveyed the inner joy that the Sabbath indeed brought to her and to the rest of the worshipers. Though living a very barren life, measured on any social scale, yet it was undeniable that the Sabbath elevated their meager lives into a joyful encounter with Jesus and fellow worshippers. That is the blessing of the Sabbath, a sanctuary in time for the soul.

The over-crowded schedules that baffle most people throughout the week is a fixture of life today. On a good week, by Thursday, we are exhausted. But for Seventh-day Adventist Christians, we know that it is soon to be Sabbath—a haven of peace, relaxation with family, and time to refocus. In our family, Friday evenings are a delight. We gather leisurely in the family room and share what we consider to be the biggest blessing of the week. As we listen and embrace the experiences, we are all drawn closer in a spirit of gratitude and thanksgiving. Then we go around the room and make known our prayer requests. That is followed by prayer, after which we embrace and wish each other a happy Sabbath. According to the season of the year, a light supper may follow. We experience a serene camaraderie along with sweet fellowship. The evening is joyous and emits a wonderful sense of peace and wholeness.

---

indestructible refuge from time's insatiable silent rush that traps us all in its unrelenting flow. Called the Sabbath, it has its origin in the foundation of the world itself—that is, it was part of the original Creation, something as primeval and basic as time itself, because it is part of time." Clifford Goldstein, *Life Without Limits: Powerful Truths for Your Journey to Hope and Meaning* (Hagerstown, MD.: Review and Herald Publishing Association, 2007), 153. Former United States Senator, Joseph Lieberman, a very busy man for sure, has written how he carved out the Sabbath hours in his scheduling so as to be home with his family on Friday evening and the entire Sabbath. It is motivational to read how precious little would keep him away from the Sabbath experience. Joseph Lieberman, *The Gift of Rest: Rediscovering the Beauty of the Sabbath* (New York: Howard Books, 2011).

The experience is continued on the Sabbath day. After worship, the highlight of the day, the family comes together for the Sabbath meal. It is usually special in some fashion, and it tastes exceedingly gratifying. Time is spent in wholesome family time, nature walks, reading, and/or special visits to individuals needing a special emotional lift. For us, the Sabbath is indeed the best day of the week. At the end of the Sabbath hours, we do feel refreshed and rejuvenated. We sense that we will be OK as we begin to get ready for another grinding week, knowing and expecting that once again, the Sabbath will halt our schedules and embrace us with its exhilarating twenty-four hours.

Church Finances: When it comes to finances, money is usually scarce at every level of church administration. It happens even during times of economic upturns. So, the economic cycles are not entirely the culprit for the lack of funds. The quandary merely points to a lackluster level of commitment by the membership or improper allocation of the funds. In some instances, top-heavy organizations are guilty of siphoning much-needed funding that would otherwise go to keep the main thing, the main thing.[27]

When Haggai was called to his prophetic ministry, the would-be temple builders were primarily engaged in fixing their homes and making a living. They were undaunted by the fact that the temple remained unfinished. Yet, their homes were becoming outlandishly impressive while the temple languished in disrepair (see Hag. 1:2–4). There are strident similarities between that scene and today's church. Laodicea boasts, "I am rich; I have acquired wealth and do not need a thing" (Rev. 3:17). Since we are living in the time frame of the Laodicean church, a portion of that sobering

---

[27]George R. Knight, *The Fat Lady and the Kingdom: Adventist mission confronts the challenges of institutionalism and secularization* (Boise, ID.: Pacific Press Publishing Association, 1995), 11–35. There are three choice quotes from the cited material that I would like to underscore: "I fear that in too many cases the church and its institutions have become a 'jobs program' and that institutional survival has become an end in itself." "There is something definitely wrong when the church falls into the role of furthering the mission of semiautonomous institutions rather than those institutions furthering the mission of the church." "Reevaluation and revolution must put mission back on the center stage, if we are to stem the drift toward dysfunctionality. The self-image of Adventism needs to be refocused on mission rather than on packages [institutions]."

message is for us. Woe unto those who are hoarding means while Jerusalem, the church of God on earth, is not being built.

That is not to say that there is no sacrificial giving. What I am saying is that it is not always proportionate to the capacity and the blessings. I have witnessed both ends of that spectrum, wealthy individuals who are not moved by glaring financial needs and folks living from paycheck to paycheck who are quick to give beyond their means. While engaged in a fund-raising campaign for a church building at my very first church, I was moved to see the level of sacrificial giving. One Sabbath, Elba (not her real name) and her family called me aside and handed to me a heavy container with all sorts of monies. There were coins and bills. It was a very significant amount of money for that family, and it seemed that it was what they had been putting aside for a rainy day. I was moved and reminded of the Macedonian believers who gave beyond their capacity (see 2 Cor. 8:1–5). Yes, there are individuals who are giving substantially to the cause of God and are being a blessing to many facets of the work. Blessings to all of your kind!

Revival Needed: Many of us are acquainted with beautiful structures of worship that have had rich and glorious histories. They are monuments to the faith of a bygone generation that united faith and funds to erect imposing buildings. Sadly, however, it seems that as the building has aged, the moving of the Holy Spirit has also languished. The magnificent edifice remains, but the moving of God is barely sensed. Quite obviously, it is not enough to have a beautiful and historic structure and live off the memories of the good old days. Such settings are in desperate need of a revival of primitive godliness. To achieve that, the Spirit must find willing hearts where He can initiate the revival. Slowly, others will join, and the cycle will repeat and expand. When that will happen, and it will, the Spirit will once again move within those settings with compelling force and results.

Conversely, there are run-down structures where people converge two or three times a week. The edifice offers precious little in the arena of comfort. The lighting is poor, the audio shrieks, and the technology is elementary. The seats are harsh and uncomfortable. Yet, in any given service, there is a sizable crowd. Why do they go? Because in that austere environment, they sense God's presence. In all honesty, wouldn't you want to be there as well? We need to be in a place where God's presence is sensed and felt. In such spiritual hotbeds, we will not only be taught of the Lord but be refashioned by the Spirit as well. Sermons are limited as to how far they can move a congregation; the inner and greater work must be done by the Holy Spirit moving upon willing believers. Yet, the worshippers need to be brought to the point of sensing their needs and thus seek the Spirit.

Within that crude and uncomfortable setting in Jerusalem, the audience was brought to the point of introspection and consequently repentance. Thus, the heart was made right for the Holy Spirit to move in and bring reformation. We urgently need such a moving of the Spirit as on that day.

Nehemiah was a bold and tenacious leader. With his skill set he was able to achieve awesome changes in a community that desperately needed them. However, what capped the physical construction of the walls of Jerusalem was the spiritual revival that broke out soon thereafter. How did it happen? Who were the main characters? Did it have lasting power? Could it happen today? It was not a revival series by the most gifted orator of the day. Not at all. It was a very simple reading of Scripture by their local pastor—Ezra. Jesus assured His followers that His words usher life (see John 6:63). When God's people have prioritized and given centrality to the Scripture, great things have happened. Every congregation needs to be fed with solid biblical teaching that not only will stir the people but will also move them to further study. A staple of every reformation has been the centrality of solid Bible teaching.[28] We need to get back to the Bible and make it central in our spiritual diet.[29]

---

[28] "We are sent not to preach sociology but salvation; not economics but evangelism; not reform but redemption; not culture but conversion; not progress but pardon; not new social order but the new birth; not revolution but regeneration; not renovation but revival; not resuscitation but resurrection; not a new organization but a new creation; not democracy but the gospel; not civilization but Christ. We are ambassadors; not diplomats." Quoted in Bert Beverly Beach, *Vatican II: Bridging the Abyss* (Washington, D.C.: Review and Herald Publishing Association, 1968), 148.

[29] "Yes, our people are hungry to hear the great truths that have made us a special people, and well they might be. Many of them have given up much in the way of family relationships

Prayer also plays a central role in revival. One is made keenly aware of the dependence of Nehemiah on prayer as he gives us snapshots of his prayer life. He was a man of constant prayer and untiring action. He prayed far longer than the duration of the project itself. He prayed for the Jerusalem project for four months while the project was completed in fifty-two days. Every revival of history has been initiated by the study of the Word accompanied by heartfelt prayers. Again, that is part of the template for revival.

> *Become an agent of change—work toward revival.*

These activities—solid Biblical study and heart-felt prayer—can be done at every local church. It does not even require a budget. It does not demand a visiting pastor to conduct it. It can be done at your local congregation inexpensively, and yet it can radically change the course of that church. If the Spirit were to move upon the church in Uganda or Guam, it would not necessarily be a blessing to your local congregation. To impact your local church, the spark of revival needs to be generated there—in your local setting. Become an agent of change—work toward revival.

May we all work to that end, to fully and completely build up God's church. As a church, we have been blessed with many gifts and resources. We already have the *goods*; now we need the *Godliness*.

---

and financial gain in order to become Seventh-day Adventists. They need to be encouraged and built up in this faith, which has cost them something, but the principle is still wider. To be a Christian in this world requires a break from the world, a war with the devil, and a new life that must be constantly sustained or else it will die. So it is that all Christians need to be continually fed with spiritual food." H. M. S. Richards, *Feed My Sheep*, (Washington, D.C.: Review and Herald Publishing Association,1958), 206.

Afterthoughts

At the beginning of the Book of Ezra, Israel is captive in the land of the enemy. However, by overcoming what seemed to be an impossibility, by the end of the narrative in the book of Nehemiah, the people of God are safely back in their homeland. They have rebuilt Jerusalem and are experiencing a new beginning in the land of their ancestry. The future appears promising.

That is a fitting description of the future that awaits the Adventist believer. Today, we are engaged in the mission of expanding the church's sphere of influence in every region of the globe. Yet, when Jesus comes, we shall all be gathered from the four corners of the world as one people. Nevertheless, at the end of the Book—the Bible—God's people are within the safety of the walls of salvation and security imparted by the New Jerusalem. The days of building up Jerusalem are over; it will be a time to delight in its beauty and safety.

> When the LORD brought back the captives to Zion,
> we were like men who dreamed.
> Our mouths were filled with laughter,
> our tongues with songs of joy.

Then it was said among the nations,
"The LORD has done great things for them."
The LORD has done great things for us,
and we are filled with joy.
Restore our fortunes, O LORD,
like streams in the Negev.
Those who sow in tears
will reap with songs of joy.
He who goes out weeping,
carrying seed to sow,
will return with songs of joy,
Carrying sheaves with him.
(Psalm 126, NIV, 1984)

Fellow believer, let's build up Jerusalem. Let's finish the mission. Let's go home!

Appendix A
Chronology

Note: Although the general range of these dates is accepted within the scholarly community, there are differing viewpoints as to their exact location within the timeline. Thus, the purpose of this chronology is to set in sequence the events discussed in this work, rather than adamantly claim the exactitude of these dates.

539/538: Babylon falls, Persian Empire begins

537/536: Cyrus allows Jews to return to Jerusalem

- 50,000 exiles embark on the first wave of their homeward trek
- Zerubbabel is the political leader, and Joshua the spiritual leader
- Arrived, organized housing, and in the Fall, assembled to discuss the project

Spring 535: Construction on the temple begins

- Construction halted, the older generation which had seen former Temple, is disappointed

Chronology

- Discouragement sets in; many simply went back to their family affairs
- Leadership (Zerubbabel & Joshua) is discouraged and hard-pressed

535—521: Construction of temple and city nonexistent; people work on their homes

520: Haggai bursts unto the scene and raises the morale of the repatriates

- Zechariah chimes in and reinforces Haggai's message
- Work begins anew on the temple with renewed passion, it moves forward rapidly

515: Temple dedicated; a huge milestone achieved

515—458: Gradually, normalcy sets in; return to a passive and meager existence

Note: Not much information is available as to what occurred after the completion of the temple and the intervening 58 years till 457 BC. The prevailing silence seems to indicate that the people simply went back to a passive—mission accomplished—attitude. That generation may have passed away and the newer generation followed in their passivity until …

457: In Susa, Ezra is granted permission to go to Jerusalem and follow up on the project

- Arrived with approximately 8,000 settlers; second wave of returnees
- Tackles lingering issues that had not been resolved—e.g.: marriages with non-Jews
- Re-ignited the spiritual component among the settlers

456 Spring; wives and children who were non-Jews were asked to leave the city

444 Nehemiah arrives as governor with third wave of returnees;

- Walls are begun and completed in fifty-two days
- A movement of reform and reformation ignites amongst the people.

432 Nehemiah returns to Susa after serving in Jerusalem for twelve years

Bibliography

Beach, Bert Beverly. *Vatican II: Bridging the Abyss.* Washington, D.C.: Review and Herald Publishing Association, 1968.

Dillard, Raymond B. and Tremper Longman III, *An Introduction to the Old Testament.* Grand Rapids, MI.: Zondervan, 1994.

Edersheim, Alfred. *The Life and Times of Jesus the Messiah.* McClean, VA.: Macdonald Publishing Company, 1883.

Gaustad, Edwin Scott, ed., *The Rise of Adventism: A Commentary on the Social and Religious Ferment of Mid-Nineteenth Century America.* San Francisco: Harper and Row, Publishers, 1974.

Gladden, Ron. *Plant the Future: So Many Churches! Why Plant More?* Nampa, ID.: Pacific Press Publishing Association, 2000.

Goldstein, Clifford. *Life Without Limits: Powerful Truths for Your Journey to Hope and Meaning.* Hagerstown, MD.: Review and Herald Publishing Association, 2007.

Knight, George R. *The Fat Lady and the Kingdom: Adventist Mission Confronts the Challenges of Institutionalism and Secularization.* Boise, ID: Pacific Press Publishing Association, 1995.

Knight, George R. *Millennial Fever and the End of the World: A Comprehensive Survey of Millerism and America's Fascination with the Millennium in the Nineteenth Century.* Boise, ID.: Pacific Press Publishing Association, 1993.

Lieberman, Joseph. *The Gift of Rest: Rediscovering the Beauty of the Sabbath.* New York: Howard Books, 2011.

Maxwell, C. Mervyn. *God Cares*, 2 Vols: *The Message of Daniel for you and your Family.* Vol. 1. Boise, Idaho: Pacific Press Publishing Association, 1981.

McConville, J. G. *Ezra, Nehemiah, and Esther.* Philadelphia: The Westminster Press, 1985.

Nichol, F. D., ed. *Seventh-day Adventist Bible Commentary.* Vol. 3. Washington, DC: Review and Herald Publishing Association, 1953–1957.

Richards, H. M. S. *Feed My Sheep*, Washington, D.C.: Review and Herald Publishing Association,1958.

Swindoll, Charles R. *Hand Me Another Brick: How Effective Leaders Motivate Themselves and Others.* Nashville, TN: Thomas Nelson, Inc. 1998.

Seventh-day Adventist Church Manual. Hagerstown, MD.: Review and Herald Publishing Association, 2000.

White, Ellen G. *The Acts of the Apostles.* Mountain View, CA.: Pacific Press Publishing Association, 1911.

TEACH Services, Inc.
P U B L I S H I N G

We invite you to view the complete
selection of titles we publish at:
www.TEACHServices.com

We encourage you to write us
with your thoughts about this,
or any other book we publish at:
info@TEACHServices.com

TEACH Services' titles may be purchased in
bulk quantities for educational, fund-raising,
business, or promotional use.
bulksales@TEACHServices.com

Finally, if you are interested in seeing
your own book in print, please contact us at:
publishing@TEACHServices.com

We are happy to review your manuscript at no charge.

www.ingramcontent.com/pod-product-compliance
Lightning Source LLC
Chambersburg PA
CBHW070544170426
43200CB00011B/2544